Athene Series
Feminist Scholarship on
Culture and Education

**Privilege in the
Medical Academy**
*A Feminist Examines Gender,
Race, and Power*
Delese Wear

**Re-Engineering Female
Friendly Science**
Sue V. Rosser

All the Rage
*Reasserting Radical Lesbian
Feminism*
Lynne Harne & Elaine Miller,
Editors

**Creating an Inclusive
College Curriculum**
*A Teaching Sourcebook from
the New Jersey Project*
Ellen G. Friedman, Wendy K.
Kolmar, Charley B. Flint, and
Paula Rothenberg, Editors

Teaching the Majority
*Breaking the Gender Barrier
in Science, Mathematics, and
Engineering*
Sue V. Rosser, Editor

The Will to Violence
The Politics of Personal Behavior
Susanne Kappeler

Crucial Conversations
*Interpreting Contemporary
American Literary
Autobiographies by Women*
Jeanne Braham

**Women's Studies
Graduates**
The First Generation
Barbara F. Luebke &
Mary Ellen Reilly

**Men Who Control
Women's Health**
*The Miseducation of
Obstetrician-Gynecologists*
Diana Scully

The Transsexual Empire
The Making of the She-Male
Janice G. Raymond

**Surviving the Dalkon
Shield IUD**
*Women v. the Pharmaceutical
Industry*
Karen Hicks

Making Violence Sexy
Feminist Views on Pornography
Diana E. H. Russell, Editor

Father Knows Best
*The Use and Abuse of Power in
Freud's Case of Dora*
Robin Tolmach Lakoff &
James C. Coyne

Keepers of the History
*Women and the Israeli-
Palestinian Conflict*
Elise G. Young

Living by the Pen
Early British Women Writers
Dale Spender, Editor

The Knowledge Explosion
*Generations of Feminist
Scholarship*
Cheris Kramarae &
Dale Spender, Editors

All Sides of the Subject
Women and Biography
Teresa Iles, Editor

Calling the Equality Bluff
Women in Israel
Barbara Swirski &
Marilyn P. Safir, Editors

Black Feminist Criticism
*Perspectives on Black Women
Writers*
Barbara Christian

The Writing or the Sex?
*or why you don't have to read
women's writing to know it's no
good*
Dale Spender

Narodniki Women
*Russian Women Who Sacrificed
Themselves for the Dream of
Freedom*
Margaret Maxwell

Speaking Freely
*Unlearning the Lies of the
Fathers' Tongues*
Julia Penelope

**The Reflowering of the
Goddess**
Gloria Feman Orenstein

Female-Friendly Science
*Applying Women's Studies
Methods and Theories to
Attract Students*
Sue V. Rosser

Privilege in the Medical Academy

A FEMINIST EXAMINES GENDER, RACE, AND POWER

Delese Wear

FOREWORD BY FRANCES K. CONLEY

Teachers College, Columbia University
New York and London

Published by Teachers College Press, 1234 Amsterdam Avenue, New York, NY 10027

Library of Congress Cataloging-in-Publication Data

Wear, Delese.
    Privilege in the medical academy : a feminist examines gender, race, and power / Delese Wear ; foreword by Frances K. Conley.
        p.   cm.—(Athene series)
    Includes bibliographical references and index.
    ISBN 0-8077-6290-3 (alk. paper).—ISBN 0-8077-6288-1 (pbk. : alk. paper)
    1. Medical education—Philosophy.   2. Sexism in medicine.   3. Feminist criticism.
4. Feminist theory.   5. Women in medicine.   6. Literature and medicine—Study and teaching.   7. Professional socialization.   I. Title.   II. Series.
    R737.W43   1997
    610'.71'1—dc21   97-11213

ISBN 0-8077-6288-1 (paper)
ISBN 0-8077-6290-3 (cloth)

Printed on acid-free paper
Manufactured in the United States of America

04 03 02 01 00 99 98 97   8 7 6 5 4 3 2 1

Once is not enough: the tale must be told again, and yet again.

—Vivian Gornick, "Why Memoir Now?"

Contents

Foreword

IN AN ERA of proliferative biotechnology, in which science has triumphed over art, the task of teaching of humanity to would-be doctors has moved from the traditional old-time, revered practitioner to a new breed of "medical humanists." Science reigns, and too often the current crop of academic physicians has little inclination for teaching the mundane elements of how to treat a patient with compassion; to visualize each patient as being of equal worth as a human being; to explore the depths and guts of racism, sexism, ageism, and homophobia; and to question how all of these affect the quality of care a doctor delivers. Their concerns are more with DNA, genetic encoding, T and B cells of the immune system, and how to increase the survival time of a patient after a liver transplant.

Teaching the practice of humane medicine has been turned over to new academic professionals with humanities degrees, often in literature or ethics, who enter the medical world rather tentatively, often without a defined role in a rigid hierarchy and traditional educational program. They are on the fringe of the medical academy, can never expect to be true insiders, and, as such, at times lack credibility, are treated with tolerance but not true respect, and experience trivialization of both their expertise and their endeavors. The price of admission is assimilation, but these voices will only continue to be heard if there is a rebuke of total belonging. A recounting of their struggle to reach and teach the next generation of physicians is an introspective one as they puzzle over their appropriate fit in this world they would change but one that, overall, has little desire to be changed.

Delese Wear is one such professional, and her voice is an interesting, arresting one. At her institution I am certain she is chastised for being strident, stubborn, unidimensionally feminist, not sufficiently cognizant of that hallowed medical world she works to modify to be taken seriously. And yet she believes so fervently in herself and in her ability to transform unjust social relations in medicine through awakening the hearts, minds, and souls of the next generation of doctors that we listen and we listen carefully. She is a professional engaged in a project in which critique of literature is used to explore and hopefully end the insidious, unequal social relations that are the hallmark of medicine and its practitioners.

One must be willing to confront prejudice rather than pretend it does not exist, not to accept that sheer numbers equal equity, and be willing to recognize the complexities of knowledge, language, power, and perception, and how very easy it is to make presumptions.

Much of her classroom teaching is from a feminist viewpoint, clearly stated to come from a privileged, white, educated, heterosexual female academic. Most feminist critique received in medical education is framed to keep women on the defensive, offering hope for improvement but only if the patriarchal boat is not rocked. Yet often her female students reject the "feminist" label, forcing an interesting dichotomy wherein they have gained entrance into a professional world by help from the feminist movement but subsequently define the label of "feminist" as part of a "victim" mentality that "demonizes" men. With such resistance, why project a feminist viewpoint in medical education at all?

Delese Wear convincingly argues that feminist theorizing can open eyes to all forms of oppression, prejudice, and inequality. Medical education, however, often develops the doctor as a privileged Us, patients as a lesser Them. Yet every physician must develop sufficient sensitivity to recognize ongoing societal dynamics resulting from, for example, racism, poverty, or old age in the patients he or she treats. Breaking these formidable barriers should produce a generation of physicians who at least recognize that social inequality is a major determinant in the quality of health care they themselves, as well as others, deliver.

By virtue of selection and education, doctors are privileged individuals, occupying a privileged professional place in society and often achieving a privileged financial status. A necessary dimension of working against unjust social relations is to confront and understand one's own privilege, whatever it may consist of. Through analysis of literature and by promulgating her deeply personal, introspective look into her position of "privilege," Wear asks students to consider the idea that "unlearning" one's racism or sexism is a lifelong process and the necessity of converting individual prejudice into more structural and politicized terms applicable to the whole of the profession.

Once medical students finish medical school they are lost to a narrow, focused world that swallows their time and enervates their souls. A powerful argument for inclusion of humanists in medical education is that they represent a final chance to instill a creative spark, a love for imagination, in the brains of our doctors before they are gone forever into their cloistered professional world of, yes, privilege. Fictional voices tell stories not in the dry, clinical terms that doctors hear, record, and read day in and day out but with feeling, with angst, with emotion, with vision that forces the imagination to soar, revealing every detail of the total picture of a (fictional) person's life, forcing one, at times, to walk in that imaginary person's shoes. So, too, with patients, an all-encompassing, broad focus must be maintained if social inequalities are to be recognized and entered into the equation defining appropriate care and compassion for another human being. In the final analysis, doctors need proper perspective over their professional lives—success, or even failure, must not diminish a desire to keep dreaming, both for their own sakes and for the welfare of their patients.

Frances K. Conley

Acknowledgments

I AM GRATEFUL to the following publishers who permitted me to reprint earlier versions of my own work or to quote generously from others:

"Feminist Criticism in Literature and Medicine," copyright © 1994 by Alpha Omega Alpha Honor Medical Society, reprinted by permission from *The Pharos*, Volume 57, Number 4. "Border Crossings in Medical Education," copyright © 1997 by Alpha Omega Alpha Honor Medical Society, reprinted by permission from *The Pharos*, Volume 60, Number 1.

"Breaking the Ice in Thawing Climates: Feminism in Medical Education" was originally published as "Feminism in Medical Education" in the *Journal of the American Medical Women's Association (JAMWA)*, Vol. 49, No. 2, 1994.

"Becoming Our Sources: Theorizing and Personal Narratives," © 1995 by Human Sciences Press, reprinted by permission from *Journal of Medical Humanities*, Vol. 16, No. 3.

"Beyond Silences and Scripts" appeared in *Curriculum Inquiry*, Vol. 26, No. 3, 1996.

Excerpt from "Why We Tell Stories," reprinted by permission of Louisiana State University Press from *The Need to Hold Still*, by Lisel Mueller. Copyright © 1980 by Lisel Mueller.

Excerpt from "In These Dissenting Times," in *Revolutionary Petunias & Other Poems*, copyright © 1970 by Alice Walker, reprinted by permission of Harcourt Brace & Company.

Excerpt from Alice Walker's poem, "At First," is from her collection *Good Night, Willie Lee*, © 1979 by Doubleday & Company. Reprinted by permission of Doubleday & Co.

Excerpt from Jorie Graham's poem, "The Way Things Work," is from her collection *Hybrids of Plants and of Ghosts*, © 1980 by Princeton University Press. Reprinted by permission of Princeton University Press.

Excerpts from bell hooks's "Out of the Academy and into the Streets," which is taken from a longer version, "Theory as Liberatory Practice," reprinted by permission of the Yale Journal of Law and Feminism from *The Yale Journal of Law and Feminism*, Vol. 4, No. 1, pp. 1–12.

And my personal acknowledgments:

I am graced with a work environment that must surely be one of the warmest and most supportive spots to be found. The Human Values in Medicine office is not only a place where we enact collective commitment to teaching and scholarship; it is also a place where humor and a vital sense of the ironic are essential components of our daily lives. When one's colleagues are friends, the meaning of work is transformed in wonderfully essential ways.

For their friendship and their help in so many ways, I thank Mona Adorni, Tess Jones, Nancy McDonald, and Martin Kohn.

I thank Faye Zucker for her ability to help me focus on what I was trying to say in this book. Her comments and suggestions were a critical guide to me as I wrote and revised.

I am grateful for the literal and figurative background noise of my family; their lives remind me every day of what is important to me.

Finally, I dedicate this book to my husband, Steve Broderick, in love and friendship.

1

Becoming Our Sources: Theorizing and Personal Narratives

The grounds for knowledge are fully saturated with history and social life rather than abstracted from [them]. . . . It is a delusion—and a historically identifiable one—to think that human thought could completely erase the fingerprints that reveal its production process.
—Sandra Harding, "Rethinking Standpoint Theory"

I WRITE THIS as a feminist who lives much of her life in the academy: a medical school, to be exact—a highly specialized, particularly well-insulated academy, but still part of that cluster of institutions where knowledge is (perceived to be) made, stored, disseminated, sanctioned, and censored. I write in these pages of contestations I have had and witnessed as I came to realize that the rationalist, analytic, abstracted, author-neutered discourse of 20th-century Western medicine—the academic conversation in which I was to participate as a medical educator—was not part of my speech, or at least not part of the speech I was interested in acquiring. Mostly, this language puzzled me, and even though I admired much of its conceptual elegance and theoretical complexity, I knew it was a language I would not use. It was, in the words of Magda Lewis (Lewis & Simon, 1986), a discourse not intended for me.

In the medical academy, individuals (myself included) quickly learn what must be said and done to achieve the benefits of academic success— for ourselves, for the legitimacy and status of our disciplines in the epistemic hierarchy of medicine, and for a privileged rhetorical space for creating knowledge presumed inherent to and valued by those disciplines. That is, the price for admission to the club of science is clearly assimilation (Yeatman, 1994). As a feminist teacher and writer who has not joined this discourse, I work at transformative angles to the unmistakable patriarchic ethos of the medical academy and the larger medical culture. Thus I set myself (and have been set) outside this privileged arena, "outside" being an indefinite space full of potential . . . and often trouble. At any given time as I teach, write, and serve my academic community, I am perceived as being too political, too emotional, too subjective, and never quite reasonable or distanced enough. But, like Jane Tompkins, I am "tired of the conventions that keep discussions of epistemology, or James Joyce, segregated from meditation on what is happening outside my window or inside my heart" (1989, p. 123). And while I no longer pretend that my private life has nothing to do with my professional work, I do recognize that the ideals of rationality and objectivity that have guided and validated the creation of knowledge throughout the Western philosophical tradition (and most certainly medicine) have systematically shaped the belief that emotion and subjectivity have (1) nothing to do with rationality and objectivity, and (2) a lesser status, or often no place in the process of creating and attaining knowledge.

This book contains narratives of such matters. I write this autobiographically and personally, not as a confessional to evoke sympathy or outrage, but to participate in a critical examination of medical education and medical practice. This is an activity that involves not just feminists but also public health workers, members of and advocates for ignored and underserved communities, and others from academic and clinical settings who position themselves in contradictory relationships to medical status quos. I do so to illuminate our collective yet highly localized struggles and to work collectively and collaboratively to end ways of knowing, structures of power, and distribution of resources that oppress and exploit women medically and otherwise. I write these autobiographical accounts based on my belief that "one's own life signifies" (Gornick, 1996, p. 5) and that the collective, theorized stories of women's lives are legitimate ways to produce knowledge.

Yet as I write these first sentences, I am immediately aware of the politics of epistemic legitimacy; the skepticism evoked by theorizing grounded in personal experience; the discursive pulls of the personal and immediate, and of the so-called universal and generalizable. Still, this is my language written with a specific political intent, and if I am not to be sidetracked by the gatekeepers of intellectual authority who demand that I endlessly qualify and justify slippery, contentious words and positions, if I am not to be an apologist—again—for my contradictory words, then I must get on with my stories, even as I acknowledge the inadequacies, imperfections, and materiality of the very language I use.

While there are multiple locations from which I might begin this examination of privilege in the medical academy, I selected several circumstances involving knowledge production. My first story focuses on a conflict that erupted as I read a paper at a meeting of my peers and the problems associated with contesting ideologies and styles of presentation in such settings. My second story is one of my experiences with a clinical journal's distrust of personal, openly political writing on a medical topic. Both stories are exemplars and discussions of epistemic conflicts that distract from our collective political projects to end sexist and other forms of oppression inside and outside the academy.

STORY 1

No body can escape either the imprint of culture or its gendered meanings.
—Susan Bordo, *Unbearable Weight*

The medical school where I work and Hiram College, a small liberal arts college nearby, developed, with support from the National Endowment for the Humanities, a center for literature, medicine, and the health care professions. Every year or so a group of fellows are selected—roughly half physicians, nurses, and other health care providers; the other half humanities people from philosophy, theology, literature, and history. We meet six times over the year for four to five days each session to discuss the imaginative literature fellows have been asked to read on various issues: aging, AIDS, patients, women. Since all or most of the fellows teach in medical school/hospital settings, my assignment for our last meeting was to organize a session on feminist criticism and the medical humanities. I was in the midst of writing a paper on that very subject, so I sent all the fellows a draft of the paper several weeks before the meeting so that we might use some of it as a springboard for discussion.

When the time arrived for the session I had planned, I found myself in a large conference room with many long tables that had been pushed into a very large circle rather than kept in rows auditorium-style. The 30 fellows were there, most of them looking at me or leafing through the paper as I began the session with an overview of what I had written. I had written the paper as a feminist in the medical academy engaged in a critique of our practice in the medical humanities, literature and medicine in particular, including the following: appropriation of the humanities to meet medicine's needs/ends; a racist, sexist, heterosexist, almost exclusively Western medicine and literature canon that had emerged over the past 20 years; and suspicion if not dismissal of criticism that was not author-neutered (Miller, 1991; Tompkins, 1989)—that is, repudiation of autobiographical, ideological theorizing. My intent was also to discuss how some of us in the medical humanities deal with rationalist urgings for supposedly neutral, nonpositioned, nonperspectivalist methodologies and knowledge making. In short, I was trying to enact in that session the theorizing I was urging.

What followed was my most dreaded professional nightmare. One of the participants, an engaging literature professor from a large state university, lit into my paper with his own passionate commitments; I received this as the most humiliating professional attack I had ever experienced in public or private. Deeply troubled, he challenged me to see that what I had written, according to his reading, was another militaristic, feminist reinscription of the dualisms we did so much complaining about: male/female, good/bad, white/black, objective/subjective, and so on.

Initially speechless, I started to stammer a rebuttal. I looked around the room, waiting for someone to come to my defense. One of the women would surely jump in—several had expressed positive thoughts/questions about my paper during the preceding day. But no one said a word. The room was perfectly quiet. I felt a very familiar sensation in my body, starting vaguely in the stomach but then moving quickly up into my throat. My eyes began to water. I bit the inside of my mouth ferociously to ward off what I was about to do. But I could not help myself: I cried. Not a silent sniffle, but full-blown tears, red face, runny nose, quivering lips. I was mad as hell. I was also extremely frustrated, hurt, incredulous. But mostly angry—at him, at the fellows, at this ancient ritual that I had hated since the beginning of my initiation into academic life, and, of course, angry at myself for crying in this setting. I had, in the words of Mary Russo (1986), made a spectacle of myself.

The days that followed were difficult and awkward for everyone. I was ashamed; the professor (then and now someone I call friend) suffered dreadfully about the pain he had unintentionally caused; my colleagues felt clumsy around both of us. But during the last session before we left for home, we all managed apologies in some way or another, and some of the wounds began the slow process of healing.

––––––––––

What is the value of retelling this story here? It is embarrassing to me; readers may also find it embarrassing. I told the story not because I wanted to feel embarrassed all over again, but as an exemplar of two interrelated issues: the rigidity of thought surrounding what counts in knowledge production, and the predictable enactment of the personal ambush in academic settings. That is, I tell a *personal* story here, not some abstracted version of the nature of theory, with the belief that when women share stories of their own lives, a common experience of oppression and of resistance is recognized. . . . This politicizing gives women the courage to persist in resistance, recognizing that their difficulties have not only an individual basis but also a social and political basis as well. (Welch, quoted in Lewis, 1993, p. 50)

I also tell this story to illustrate the difficulties in moving toward connected knowledge, an ideal grounded in contextuality, receptivity, theoretical rigor, and decency. Such knowledge, along with its production, has implications for *synergy,* a notion we frequently encountered years ago, a word derived from the Greek *synergos:* "working together." A simple enough concept, like its kin collaboration, co-authorship, or collegiality—but not *really* when one considers the politicized hierarchies governing medical research and scientific discourse, not to mention the written and unwritten codes governing success in the medical academy, including the systematic exclusion of dissenters. How can synergy be achieved if the rule-makers of knowledge production do not honor the disparities, variations, and divergences of how persons unlike themselves think, speak, write, theorize, make meaning and knowledge? Anna Yeatman (1994) describes it this way:

> Individuals who belong to groups which are consistently objectified by modern science—women, blacks, colonials, peasants and other groups . . . are admitted to the scientific club only as exceptions to the norm for their group. . . . They are admitted to the club of scientists only if they combine an appropriate training in the procedures of foundationalist science with the adoption of the persona of the rational sovereign subject. In adopting this persona, "minority group" scientists are always to place loyalty to "the" community of scientists over loyalty to their origins. However, if on occasion they should contravene the scientific norms of disembodied, detached proceduralism and commit an emotional excess of some kind, this will be forgiven as an inevitable flaw which confirms their status as somewhat less than real scientists—as subaltern scientists. The flaw is even required. That is, subaltern scientists are allowed to orient their science in terms of values which pertain to their origins, as long as these values are not elaborated so as to call into question and to politicize the scientific enterprise itself. (pp. 189–190)

Thus, in the medical academy, intellectual authority is rarely ascribed to those who create knowledge differently from traditional positivist methods of bench research and clinical trials, that is, those methods in which the researcher recedes behind what is created to become "disembodied spirit, universal man" (Gallop, 1988, p. 7). Within these traditional methods, it is not just poor form to get too personal in academic writing/speaking; it is downright embarrassing. Like where I started this paper.

Theorizing arising from personal experience can be a critical epistemological method of medical inquiry, but it is often perceived to be secondary and soft if not inappropriate within scientific/medical methodologies.[1] Yet when woven together with other critical projects that bring to light codified, ritualized, and often unquestioned medical practices, personal theorizing can be a transformative agent of social change in medicine.

What is personal theorizing? Nancy K. Miller describes it as a "self-narrative woven into critical argument" that unravels public/private and objective/subjective dichotomies (1991, p. 1). Indeed, for nearly 20 years much feminist theorizing has been built on the personal, as the authority of individual experience became a current forming "oppositional angles" to dominant critical positionings (p. 14). In medicine these include contestations of the way health care is provided to women everywhere, along with the poor, the uneducated, and the inarticulate; the way doctors are educated; and the way women's contributions in medicine and medical education are minimized, trivialized, and excluded. These contestations often take the form of autobiographical narratives, which do not encourage or recognize the "theoretical evacuation of the very social subjects producing it," a stance assumed by positivist epistemologies (p. 24).

So this was the first real script I had to learn to become a medical academic: to (try to) remove myself from my academic writing by covering myself with the clever, abstract theorizing of my trade. It became an exercise that made scholarly discourse unpleasant, unnatural, even frightening for me—hardly conditions for synergy. Moments of critical connection, conversation, and yes, even synergy, occur in my and others' offices, over coffee, in hallways, during rare paper presentations, in restaurants and bars, during breakfasts or late-night talks with once-a-year friends at meetings. That is, in places where the language of my personal life and my experiences is tangled with the language of feminism, theorizing, books, criticism, teaching, curriculum—in circumstances where, before I speak, I do not insert a catheter into my soul, my memory, that place where all my experiences are stored. It is in those circumstances that I can, as Miller describes it, let it show. It is there that I unconsciously ignore the personal/public dichotomy and think and speak in the fluid back-and-forth between unedited autobiography and the subject matter under discussion. It is there that sometimes I really believe that (my) experience counts in the knowledge production, that we know reality only via our representations of reality (Yeatman, 1994).

But still, in much medical discourse, certainly that which we call academic writing in medicine, the realm of the personal is coded as soft and subjective ... and devalued by the ubiquitous medical discursive management team for that reason. Even so, like Jane Gallop, I find myself always adding autobiographical bits to my writing/speaking, "not because I tend toward exhibitionism but, more important, because at times I think through autobiography: that is to say, the chain of associations that I am pursuing ... passes through things that happened to me" (1988, p. 4). When I started thinking about synergy for this chapter, I thought about what it means to work together; I thought about the prerequisite of respect for synergy to occur; I thought about crying at Hiram.

That is why I began with that story. It was quite personal. It was embarrassing. And the reason I feel embarrassed at my own attempt to speak personally even here in these pages is that, according to Jane Tompkins, "I have been conditioned to feel that way. That's all there is to it" (1989, p. 123). But I do worry about the personal as self-indulgent, even though I usually return to question why the personal is so perceived (as self-indulgent) but not the self-righteous, exclusionary posturing and semantic showing off found in so much abstract theorizing. bell hooks (1992) persistently questions, and I think rightly so, the

> production of an intellectual class hierarchy where the only work deemed theoretical is abstract, jargonistic, difficult to read, and obtaining obscure references.... A feminist theory that can do this may legitimize feminist scholarship in the eyes of the ruling patriarchy, but it undermines and subverts feminist movements. It is the purpose of such theory to divide, separate, and exclude. And because this theory continues to be used to silence, censor, and devalue various feminist theoretical voices, we cannot simply ignore it. Concurrently, despite its uses as an instrument of domination, it may also contain important ideas that could, if used differently, serve a healing function. (pp. 80–81)

A healing function: That is part of synergy. What I am trying to do, in an effort to be myself—a woman immersed in an academic project that loosely twines together feminism, pedagogy, literature, medicine, and criticism—is to insert myself more personally into my writing and speaking. I do so not as a privatized, privileged confessional; I do so not to imply that I have a fixed and coherent subjectivity from which my "knowing" spews forth. Rather, *because* I recognize that my/our subjectivities change over time and that language, social interactions, and experiences play pivotal roles in knowledge production, I attempt to bring out of the shadows more of that self, my selves that deeply influence my thinking, theorizing, writing, teaching, and attempts to work together with others; there is no place for thinking, theorizing, or making knowledge that is outside a particular location, that is outside ideology.

I want to be, finally, an indivisible, nonunitary woman who cannot, will not be constantly screening and sorting out the events, thoughts, experiences, doubts, and anger that I live in personal and public moments. I/we might be embarrassed, but such embarrassment is, Miller tells us, a "sign that it is working. . . . embarrassment blows the cover of the impersonal as a masquerade of self-effacement . . . and points to the narcissistic fantasy . . . [of] self-sufficiency we identify with Theory; notably, those of abstraction" (1991, p. 24).

Personal criticism and synergy? It can work only if the personal, with its emphasis on voice and subjectivity, is honored as a "new repertory for an enlivening cultural criticism" (Miller, 1991, p. 25). It has to do with changing the gatekeepers for intellectual and academic authority. And it has to do with opening up a free-wheeling feminist discourse (or post-colonial, or subaltern discourse—anyone positioned in a contradictory relationship to prevailing intellectual authority) in the medical academy, which challenges the very notion of interest-free knowledge by casting the light on the "authoritative, explorative, elegant, learned voice, [who] speaks and analyzes, amasses evidence, theorizes, speculates about everything—except itself. Who speaks? For what and to whom?" (Said, 1989, p. 212).

Finally, synergy has to do with the recognition that technically precise, difficult language does permit certain types of theorizing that would be impossible without it. Synergetic knowledge making also admits the unruly, private, and ideological dimensions of personal theorizing, theorizing that turns back on itself by analyzing its own production. Such synergy can be worked toward in the medical academy with our students and peers, at the conferences where we give papers, in the scholarly journals where we publish our work—and at medical humanities institutes at small liberal arts colleges tucked away in the Ohio Western Reserve.

––––––––

Feminism in academic medicine is not a critical, hotly debated issue (see Chapters 3 and 4). In fact, feminist critiques of academic medicine are sporadic, and when they do appear they are limited to a precious few journals. The reasons are varied and complicated, embedded in matters of power and entitlement in the larger U.S. culture, all reflected in how we think about and practice medical care and medical education.

According to figures compiled annually by Janet Bickel at the American Medical Women's Association (AMWA), 4 of the 127 medical schools are headed by a woman dean. In academic medicine the number of women serving as department chairs is very low: Family practice has the most, while surgery, orthopedics, public health, neurology, and otolaryngology have none (Bickel, Galbraith, & Quinnie, 1995). Internal medicine, which has some of the largest percentages of women, has only one woman department chair. The number of full professors is very low, only 16 on average per medical school compared to 155 men per school. This, of course, means that the number of women available for top positions is quite low. Also alarming is the fact that "cohort studies reveal that women faculty are not progressing at the same rate or to the same extent as men" (p. 3). Glass ceilings or sticky floors, if not outright exclusion, seem to be a predictable environmental hazard: While women are entering all specialties in greater numbers, a higher proportion of women than men enter primary care, and women's representation in surgery and most surgical subspecialties remains below 15%. Similarly, according to the Feminist Majority Foundation (1991), the fortress of medical power in the United States, the American Medical Association (AMA), has never had a woman executive officer in its 144 years and never even had a woman board member until 1989.

It is no wonder, then, that medical education research has paid little attention to feminist pedagogy/inquiry in medical education settings. It is no wonder that scholarly activity in medical education is deeply ensnared in patriarchic illusions of neutrality, distance, and authority. It is no wonder that given the positivist credo of modern medical science and its dramatic successes, the scientific method appears to offer the "best route to reliable, objective knowledge not just of matters scientific but of everything one could want to know, from what makes a car run to what makes a person happy" (Code, 1993, p. 18). It is no wonder that when the I/me flows out onto the page—it has sometimes been viewed as, well, substandard (to The Standard) because of my subjectivity and (worst sin) explicit feminist standpoint. It is no wonder that again self-doubt twines around me when I attempt to enter an academic medical discourse by "render[ing] noisy and audible all that ha[s] been silenced in phallocentric discourse" (Minh-ha, 1989, p. 37).

STORY 2

After much deliberation, I decided to send the chapter on literary images of menopause I had just finished out for review to an academic medical journal, rather than a literary or feminist one. Such manuscripts are, of course, far less likely to be published in medical journals than are traditional clinical research or review essays. But weary of sermonizing to those who already believed as I did, I decided to seek a forum where readers were direct providers of medical care to women.

The chapter, part of a larger work on women's bodies and health in literature, proposed that fictions about menopause written by women can enlarge understandings of how women variously experience this process and might be useful in the teaching of menopause to medical students and residents. This belief is characteristic of Edward Said's (1993) concept of contrapuntal reading, whereby views and experiences play off each other, intertwine and overlap, "with only a provisional privilege being given to any particular one; yet . . . there is concert and order, an organized interplay that derives from the themes" (p. 51). As they examine clinical accounts of menopause concurrently with women's fictional accounts, readers may be prompted to question how the medicalization of this biological process has deeply prescribed and limited our conceptions of menopause, thus influencing the way many Western women approach and experience it. Reading widely from poetry, short stories, novels, and autobiographical accounts of menopause, I found the experience diversely interpreted and lived as a rite or passage, a relief, a celebration, a time for reflection: a process far more unruly and multilayered than the menopause-as-deficiency-disease found in much of the medical literature.

I sent the chapter to one of the most prominent journals in primary care medicine. The editors reviewed the manuscript for the usual amount of time, and several months later I received, much to my surprise, a letter that began with that eagerly anticipated, "We are pleased to inform you . . . ." The letter went on to say, however, that before it could be published the manuscript would require revision. Then I came to the following paragraph:

> Our reviewers and editorial staff commented that some of the language used in this manuscript might be construed as opinionated, inflammatory, or hyperbolic. The comments like "ageist and consumerist," "patriarchy," "particularly troubling," "essentializing distortions," and "vacuous insinuations" are most obvious, but there are *many* other examples as well. This type of language creates the image that you are overly zealous in your presentation, and it detracts from the power of your manuscript. Please go through the paper carefully and "tone down" the language to make it sound more objective and less emotional.

I was stunned, yet I laughed and said to myself out loud, "Hell *yes*, I'm opinionated!" I waved the letter in front of my colleagues and faxed it to several physician friends, and we all had a good laugh at the patronizing naiveté of an editor who would tell an explicitly feminist author to "tone it down." But back in my office, underneath all my nonchalance, I was frustrated.

I was reminded again, first-hand, that the Western medical-scientific discourse is still the creation of a small group of highly educated, privileged, (usually) white men. I was reminded again that through their power and illusions of rationality and objectivity they could exclude "the attributes and experiences commonly associated with femaleness and underclass social status: emotion, connection, practicality, sensitivity, and idiosyncracy"—what the fictions *and* I were exhibiting (Code, 1993, p. 21). I was reminded again that they had me by the . . . what? Tongue? Pen?

Of course all this is tangled in epistemological questions of knowledge, power, and exclusion. It presents a challenge to the rationalist, objectivist belief that knowledge is something situated outside the knower, that real knowledge doesn't reflect the person who produces it. My project as a feminist teacher and researcher, looming huge and difficult before me, concerns the political struggle over meaning, the need to "examine and question self-consciously [both my students and I] the conditions of our own meaning-making and to use it as the place from which to begin to work toward change" (Lewis, 1990, p. 470). As I tried to understand the meanings my writings might have for the editors of a clinical journal, I had to consider what and how much I was willing to erase or homogenize my writing in order for my work to appear in a journal read by so many physicians who care for women.

As the days and weeks went by, my naiveté became apparent. I came to realize that just because *I* do not use a scientific-rationalist creed to think about, explain, describe, or theorize about the variously lived experiences of women's bodies and health, others obviously do. Most do, of course, in medical environments. This perspective privileging "objectivity" not only has served scientists and clinicians (and me) well in the age of modern medicine, it continues to act as the foundational gatekeeper for what counts as knowledge and what does not. Still, I assumed that my writing, in both its content and form, might be admissible, even to those who view the world primarily with a positivist epistemology, those with the power to allow certain languages and methodologies in and keep others out. I wondered if I should become multilingual, to revert back to a protective anonymity when I ventured into indifferent if not suspicious territory. I wondered under what conditions I should suppress my native and acquired tongue, and when not to. I remembered Adrienne Rich's words, "this is the oppressor's language / yet I need it to talk to you" (1984, p. 117).

At first I thought the editors' problems were with the tone and texture of my manuscript, akin to what I raised in the first story regarding personal criticism and autobiography, not the fact that I was trying to demedicalize, via fictions, a natural biological process for women. Yet the more I thought about it, the more I came to believe that it wasn't merely my first-person musings that "detracted" from the text. Perhaps the editors' problems had to do with my confronting the power associated with the medicalization of women's bodies, "based on processes of removal (incision, cutting, removing, and reduction), or addition (inlaying, stitching, injection), [which] demonstrates a body pliable to power, a *machinic* organism in which 'components' can be altered, adjusted, removed, or replaced" (Grosz, 1993, p. 199). Fictions undermine this medicalization by suggesting that there is a plurality of potential techniques, approaches, and methods within knowledges, even though currently a single or limited number of paradigms govern knowledge production in medicine. This singularity, according to Grosz, indicates power, not reason, at work. Furthermore, "this power, although not as clearly visible as other forms of patriarchal coercion, is nonetheless integral to women's containment within definitions constituted by and for men" (p. 210).

As a woman in the medical academy, my work demands connection to others. Connection, of course, is variously interpreted: connecting to students, to peers/colleagues, to readers. My problem is not one of failure to connect, but of how to connect. Ursula K. LeGuin makes this distinction:

> The essential gesture of the father tongue is not reasoning, but distancing— making a gap, a space, between the subject or self and the object or other.... Everywhere now everybody speaks [this] language in laboratories and government buildings and headquarters and offices of business.... The father tongue is spoken from above. It goes one way. No answer is expected, or heard.... The mother tongue, spoken or written, expects an answer. It is conversation. The mother tongue is language not as mere communication, but as relation, relationship. It connects. (quoted in Tompkins, 1989, p. 127)

So, given all these ruminations about subjectivity and voice and connection in the epistemic landscape, what happened to the literary images of menopause manuscript? I changed it, just the way they asked. I made a gap between myself and the text, and ultimately between the myself and the reader. But now, even when I try to justify why I purged myself and my polemics out of the manuscript (that is, to get it published), I still wonder if it was so diluted as to be ineffective, assuming it was effective originally. I wonder if, by receding behind the content into a more depoliticized, unlit corner, I allowed my work to be open for appropriation by those who continue to manage and manipulate women's biology, health, and bodies. Perhaps when I "toned down" my discussion, I sterilized the fiction itself by placing it in a more acceptable clinical format: the passivity of an inscribed menopausal body is more palatable than "desiring, inscribing bodies that . . . make their own inscriptions on the bodies of others, themselves, and the law" (Grosz, 1993, p. 199).

The questions persist.

————————

> Really,
> you've got to be kidding. Other
> women have already done this
> sort of suffering for you,
> or so I thought.
> —Alice Walker, "At First"

Now what? I want to tie all this together with hope. But how do I move away from the frustration and anger I have written about? And how far away do I move?

I want to turn back to the idea of synergy, itself full of hope, and how personal writing may promote it. Nancy K. Miller describes feminine exposure in writing, how anger is slipped into the folds of argument, and how "it's not supposed to show, but it does" (1991, p. 23). Yet when this occurs, the writer is not encapsulated in her own sorry world because of her exposed anger and the spectacle she makes of herself. Instead, "far from being turned in on itself in a miserable 'privatization of the personal,' [it] is the contrary, to bring back an old-fashioned word: engaged" (p. 24).

Engaged. It sounds like one dimension of synergy. But when I/we "let it show," is our engagement only with each other, with academic women whose projects are similar? When we move away from writing for sympathetic readers, do we expect our writing to crack open, even slightly, the rationalist certainty of editors, publishers, and peers? Do we modify our writing voices to become sonorous to those who set The Standard and whose surveillance maintains the sounds by keeping out all that is atonal and disharmonious to them?

Sandra Harding helps me think about this, about my troubles with androcentric epistemologies that often seem to thwart and discourage my efforts. She writes of me: a woman-as-knower, a creator of knowledge, someone who has participated in the construction of history, a person whose life can provide a "grounding for knowledge claims" (1991, p. 47). Yet all this seems contrary to biomedical/academic medicine's knowledge claims: It is not in keeping with what it means to be scientific, and I am *not* "dispassionate, disinterested, impartial, concerned with abstract rules" (p. 47). However, my purpose is not to trash the reformative, progressive inclinations of modern Western science that have given me and many women a healthier and easier life, but only its oppressive, exploitive tendencies that often go unchallenged or unacknowledged. I want to demonstrate that reason and emotion are not in opposition but rather are "mutually constitutive" and that the ideal of detached inquiry is an "impossible dream . . . or perhaps a myth that has exerted enormous influence on Western epistemology. Like all myths, it is a form of ideology that fulfills certain social and political functions" (Jaggar, 1992, p. 128).

Moreover, what I want as part of a community engaged in critical inquiry in the medical academy is not to be placed at epistemic disadvantage in the larger medical and scientific discourse because the knowledge/methodological claims I and others make are in opposition to context-independent criteria of legitimization. I want to be able to start from the dailiness of our lives, which may lead to different understandings of the diversity of lived experiences and of the various ways to make knowledge and meaning. Bettina Aptheker writes:

> By the dailiness of women's lives I mean the patterns women create and the meanings women invent each day and over time as a result of their labors and in the context of their subordinated status to men. . . . The point is to suggest a way of knowing from the meanings women give to their labors. The search for dailiness is a method of work that allows us to take the patterns women create and the meanings women invent and learn from them. If we map what we learn, connecting one meaning or invention to another, we begin to lay out a different way of seeing reality. This way of seeing is what I refer to as women's standpoint. (quoted in Harding, 1991, p. 129)

The "we" in "we map" seems especially important to me as I try to justify spending such a significant part of my life writing to/for other academic women in scholarly journals or at meetings attended by others whose lives resemble mine is so many ways. This inclusive "we" is why I usually feel so (tenderly) provoked, stirred, and moved to action when I read other women's scholarly writing. Yes, I am privileged and white and most of the other predictable disclaimers, but I am engaged in a project to end the insidious, unequal social relations found virtually everywhere in contemporary U.S. culture, inequalities that translate directly into the quality of health care a person receives. Connecting to others' similar projects, often via passive reading or listening to these known and unknown peers, keeps me thinking, committed, and sustained in my hope that I don't need to hide or renounce the way I think, write, and teach for social change. Such ongoing connections, linked yet admittedly removed from the lives of most women outside the academy, can be synergetic.

But this synergy can be elitist and exclusionary. When I read what I have just written about academic projects, I realize, uneasily, how much it sounds like the familiar "Us doing for Them." I realize, uneasily, that adding the personal, political, and local to the epistemic arena does not necessarily displace the elitist and exploitive nature often associated with Western scientific rationality and neutrality. I think of bell hooks, who has been moving about in various worlds linking theorizing to processes of self-recovery and collective liberation, and who reminds us that theorizing is not "inherently healing, liberatory, or revolutionary" (1992, p. 80). She points out that even within the domain of personal or autobiographical writing, we often find work that is filled with feminist idiom, is difficult to read, and is full of obscure or cryptic references that only the widely read feminist scholar would catch. This writing is not widely synergetic. In fact, she claims that one of the uses of such writing is the construction and maintenance of an "intellectual class hierarchy" (1992, p. 80), which clearly leaves out most women. She writes:

> I find writing—theoretical talk—to be most meaningful when it invites readers to engage in critical reflection and in the practice of feminism. To me, this theory emerges from my efforts to make sense of everyday life experiences, efforts to critically intervene in my life and the lives of others. This to me is what makes feminist transformation possible. Personal testimony, personal experience, is such fertile ground for the production of liberatory feminist theory.... While we work to resolve those issues that are most pressing we engage in a critical process of theorizing that enables and empowers. (1992, pp. 81–82)

Theorizing that includes reflection, everyday life experiences, and hope for intervention and change: This includes much of the ground of sense making for me and many other women who are committed to a broad-based feminist movement, not one that only the privileged engage in during work hours in the academy.

The hope I have for such theorizing brings me back to where I started. Nothing much has changed since I started writing this: I am silenced, but more often I choose silence as an act of revolt (Lewis, 1993). I hear and see rewarded recitations of medicalized scripts that offer totalizing explanations of the world, but I find purpose and meaning in the fluid, open-ended scripts of feminist theorizing. I still work in a rationalist, male-dominated, sometimes misogynist academy, and I still want my work to appear in those journals read by medical educators and providers of medical care to women; I and my colleagues still measure my identity and worth in relation to these sanctioned discourses. But as I read, think, and write, I find myself nourished by the implied readers of these pages, other women whose work may have deepened and enlarged my understandings of the various feminisms and the meanings of scholarship, and who, as they read here, listen to me. Yes, I will continue to send my work to those editors who may appropriate it even as they set restrictive critical standards, but I will also look to other approaches to conversation that take me "out of the academy and into the streets" (hooks, 1992, p. 80). Such a subaltern effort—I think, I hope, I am counting on—could be productive ground for the creation of a synergetic, more inclusive, liberatory feminist theorizing.

It is what I am working toward as I write this very book.

2

Beyond Silences and Scripts: The Variety of Feminist Experience

I wear my skin only as thin as I have to, armor myself only as seems absolutely necessary.

—Dorothy Allison, *Skin*

I AM IN the back of one of those kitschy horse and carriages in Charleston, South Carolina. We just bought our tickets, found some iced coffee, and slid into the back seat for a 45-minute tour of the historic Battery district. Two families with children join the three of us. Our guide is a handsome, pony-tailed college student named Troy. This is his summer job; the rest of the year he studies music. He tells us that he sings and composes, and that his influences are Dan Fogelberg, the Eagles, and John Denver. He is friendly and witty, and I like him.

I sit there looking at him, wondering what he thinks about the Shannon Faulkner "situation." He surely must have an opinion on her resignation from The Citadel—the all-male military school she recently won the legal right to attend as a full-time cadet. I have been in Charleston several days now, first tentatively, now relentlessly asking people I meet—food servers, shopkeepers, the concierge in our hotel—what they think of her resignation after only one week of classes, the result of her emotional exhaustion from a two-year legal ordeal. Those I have asked so far have all responded with a toned-down version of the gleefully venomous response given by many of The Citadel's male cadets when they heard that she had resigned. No one, not one person I have asked, gives the brave Ms. Faulkner much understanding or support.

I catch Troy's eye and ask, "So. What do you think of what went on at The Citadel with Shannon Faulkner?" He has obviously thought about it. Through his charming smile, he vehemently argues that she *should* have been expected to do everything required of her male counterparts ("if you can't take the heat . . . ") and continues talking to me and the

17

others about the price of equality and the virtues of single-sex institutions. His talk becomes background as I stop listening and silently start to compose a list of all the reasons he is so, so wrong. But as I look around the carriage, I see my relaxed companions, none of them looking for anything more than an effortless exchange with a stranger, certainly not the serious positioning of political argument.

I sigh and say nothing. I think of all the good reasons not to respond to what he said. The old cliché about *choosing* one's battles. My friends' and colleagues' frequent weariness with my relentless feminist vigilance . . . my predictable, scripted responses, they say. Knowing he is no more likely to listen to me than I am to him. Not wanting to annoy the others in the carriage. Not wanting to ruin these sweet moments with my friends in this beautiful old city. And besides all that, what would be the point of responding in that context?

I let the moment pass, but the urge returns later in the day and I start asking again. The young woman in Bath and Body Works—a college student with an open sociology text by the cash register—wonders about the point Ms. Faulkner was really trying to make and then starts mumbling unhappily about the dissolution of gender.

The concierge responds through fixed smile and unfaltering politeness another nonanswer, something about oh yes that's quite the news again these days, then quickly moves on to safer ground with directions on how to get to a movie theater.

As we pass a young college student selling walking tours of Charleston, I have a thought that she might give a response mirroring mine. (Was I purposefully looking for young people, assuming they'd be less rigid about gender roles?) Wrong again. She grins and tells us she knows lots of guys from The Citadel and they certainly didn't want Faulkner there. Still smiling, she tells us about the "Save the Males" bumper stickers that had appeared all over Charleston during the past several years. We walk away, and I still don't know what she thinks.

What is the point here anyway? I wonder again. Why my need to question all these people, these strangers? Is it a need to position myself publicly or to show off intellectually, like wearing a name tag with my title on it? Anatole Broyard (1992), *The New York Times* literary critic who chronicled his own illness and dying, told the story about Proust wanting his doctor to know that he had read Shakespeare. I sit in the carriage and want these others to know that I am a feminist.

But what do these random responses from strangers mean? To me? To Shannon Faulkner? To larger struggles to end oppressions based on race or age, gender or social class, nationality or sexual desire? Without a willingness to enter a discussion with Troy (and others) across our very substantial differences, shouldn't I have just kept my mouth shut in the first place? Why raise the issue and then leave it without a word? Doesn't my silence make me complicitous? I think of Patricia Williams's ruminations on silence, her own, even in the presence of others' racist remarks; such silence that is "too common, too institutionalized, and too destructive not to examine it in the most nuanced way possible" (1991, p. 127). And the price—always high—of speaking up, the clichéd charges of being "overly sensitive . . . touchy . . . of building walls, of being unrealistic, of not being able to loosen up and just be with people" (p. 125).

Or maybe this is a kind of ideological voyeurism, except that I (the voyeur) get no kick from others' personal disclosures. Or maybe I am masochistic, inviting this one-way neoconservative volley. But wait. Perhaps I do get some kind of sorry, self-righteous pleasure from all this: "these people" without a highly developed social conscience (like mine) and the world "they" reproduce fuel my life's work. Without sexism, what would I *do*?

———————

And now what? Unless this is to turn into self-indulgent confession, I better find some theoretical thread to weave back through or around this story and the ones that follow, to tie them together or pull them along. Telling stories is never enough, is it? Even though I write as an act of inclusion, to provide companionship in a collective struggle, to offer encouragement in a sexist academic environment that fosters aggression and competition, I still must "do theory" in some kind of way. Shouldn't I? Perhaps it is my conception of theorizing as an explicit elevation of thought to a more abstract level that seems absent from the dailiness of stories I tell, even if these stories are saturated with social and political content.

"You go to the priesthood to get the tools," says Molly Hite (1993), but I'm not sure what the tools of doing theory are these days, and while I don't have the need to be accepted by the Great Father anymore, I do seek approval of the Great Mother. Is this OK, Mom? Am I doing it right? Is this too self-absorbed, too naive? Is this theorizing?

No answers. Rather, what I witness and participate in (right here) is what Gayle Greene describes as "turning in on ourselves with this fierce self-scrutiny [which is] a form of self-erasure, an analogue to our obsession with thinness, a way of assuring ourselves and others that we'll take up less space—a kind of professional/pedagogical anorexia" (1993, p. 17).

Is this theorizing now that I've moved above my story to look down upon it and sprinkled it with the observations of others?

> Unanalyzed pain leads us to numbness, subservience, or to random and ineffectual bursts of violence. As separate individuals, women have rarely been in a position to use our pain and anger as a creative force for change. Most women have not even been able to touch this anger, except to drive it inward like a rusted nail.
>
> —Adrienne Rich, "Disloyal to Civilization"

We walk into the conference room, and the nine of them are already there—directors of medical education at our eight teaching hospitals, and the dean of our medical school. You've seen the setup before: a small windowless room with a rectangular table surrounded by a dozen or so chairs. We ease into two empty chairs at the end of the table near the door, and after a brief introduction by the dean, we begin. I am pleased that the dean shows more than a "that's nice, girls" attitude toward our program and is willing to match his words with deeds.

"We" are two women in our forties, white, one MD, one PhD. I am a faculty member in the behavioral sciences department, and my partner is a family doctor who is the director of Women in Medicine for the college of medicine where we teach. Our companions at the table are all men, all white, several PhDs but mostly MDs. Our task is to tell them about the history of the Women in Medicine program at the college, its present focus, and the goals we have for the program. We are talking to them because one of our goals involves refocusing more of our efforts from the preclinical, college-based setting to the hospitals where our young doctors learn clinical medicine and where much of the overt sexism in medicine occurs. It is there where students confront the most flagrant sexual/sexist "humor," banter, and intimidation. It is there where the specialty sorting kicks in, with women (and minority men) still turned away from many of the prestigious, exclusionary subspecialties. It is there where women begin to face difficult lifestyle decisions: specialty choices, if and when to have a child during their training, how to balance their professional work and their lives outside medicine.

We explain our plan to them: to recruit a woman physician in each teaching hospital who is willing to be a mentor and advocate for women students. Such an advocate, we argued, would be far more useful to medical students than the two of us are at the centralized, geographically distant Women in Medicine office at the medical school. Furthermore, such a person would be familiar with the formal/informal structures and political networks in her particular hospital. Her immediate presence and (we hope) secure position would make her an ally for women students seeking advice or help.

The first shot is fired. (I do not choose this metaphor lightly; this was an act of aggression.) One of the physicians who has been waiting impatiently interrupts me with a comment he's been suppressing all afternoon, perhaps all his life. Nearly clenching his teeth, enunciating each word, he looks at us sternly and says, "Almost 50% of our classes are women. *Why do we need a Women in Medicine program? Why not a Men in Medicine program?*" (emphasis his).

I am incredulous. Who would have believed that this accomplished man, who had devoted his life to taking care of sick people and teaching medical students, could confuse sheer numbers with equity? After a great deal of stammering, I collect myself enough to answer, "Well, I, too, will support a Men in Medicine program [as if one did not already exist, I thought] after a few things are cleared up. If you'll look around the room, you'll notice that there are nine white men sitting around this table. Nine positions, nine men. If you'll think of the department chairs, division chiefs, and program directors in your hospitals and here at the medical school, you'll notice that they are almost exclusively men. If you'll look at the figures nationally: 126 medical schools, and only 4 women deans?" My fury rising, I stopped myself even though I could have gone on. I know this stuff; I can crunch numbers with the best of them if that's what they want. But it was comeback time, and I'd stepped way, way out of bounds in this setting.

The first response: "It's just that kind of incendiary rhetoric that turns potential allies off . . . " (What he meant to say: "You're not being nice enough.") Another response: "We don't need a Women in Medicine program at our hospital. We've got a group of banshees there . . . any of us get out of line, you see tomahawks whizzing by . . . these gals are tough . . . they take no prisoners." (What he meant to say: "Feminists are out of control." What he also unwittingly showed us was his bigotry.) Another response: "If you think you can just ride in on your white horses and tell us what's wrong . . . well . . . that's not going to happen." (What he meant to say: "We decide if and when there'll be change here.")

Scripts are flying all over the room in all directions. Mine emanate from my own experiences fused with my understandings of feminist theory. What about the others? Were their scripts written in the same way? Had these powerful men in medicine ever examined their own privileges rather than assuming them as merited entitlements? Policy makers in medical education—overwhelmingly male, white, economically privileged—reside in institutions designed by and for people just like them. The 20th century has been good to them: U.S. medicine is formidable here and around the world. It confers enormous power and privilege on those who govern it and those who practice it. But U.S. medicine, to borrow from Virginia Woolf's statement about science, "is not sexless; she is a man, a father, and infected too" (quoted in Holmes, 1992, p. 2). If the deans in this room examined the lay of the medical land more closely, they would see and understand what it means to and for them and other powerholders that women do more than 90% of the "hands-on sick care: feeding, bathing, cleaning up (vomit, feces, urine, mucus, blood), providing comfort, raising morale. Any infection of the health care system also poisons the caregivers" (Holmes, p. 3). They would also see that their position is possible *because* of the hierarchies, the line and staff relationships, the strict codes of behavior, spheres of influence, and practice arenas firmly demarcated within the institution—by them and their look-alike predecessors. They benefit socially, economically, and politically from the status quo; *women* in medicine (read: any group other than those presently inhabiting such spaces) have the potential to change, however slowly, both the system and the recipients of its rewards.

In the midst of all this, the dean leaves, and the two of us become invisible as all discussion takes place between and among the eight men as they attempt to figure out what to do with all this, assuring each other that women really don't have a "problem" at their hospitals.

Father knows best, I remind myself, and language fails me again as I sit there gnawing on the inside of my mouth, fighting back rage, wondering how I had gotten myself into this, swearing never to do it again.

Silence, again. But later I tell the dean that I will not participate in this sanctioned violence again. I tell him I will continue to enact my feminist commitments in their various forms in my teaching, my research, and my service to the college. (Now I think back on how silly "enacting my feminist commitments" sounds, as if it were a specific set of behaviors I can just pull out. My feminism is part of everything that makes me myself: my academic self, my professor self, my friend self, my wife self, my mother self, my daughter self.[1]) I leave his office feeling self-righteous but recognize, uneasily, that when I find myself in similar circumstances—which I most certainly will as an academic woman—all the old fears of past violation and subordination will likely recur, along with my silence. But maybe not. Is it possible that if we learn to disclose our dangerous memories, which Magda Lewis (1993) calls the "basis of our collective consciousness of resistance, subversion, and political change," we advance a practice that hears women's silence and makes out of it a "discourse directed toward change"? (1993, pp. 9, 3)

I take this experience out, examine it again, write it down, and search for new meanings, even as I know that my understandings of everything that has happened to me pass through my historical, social, and cultural being, *and* my language; these come before me and form me, even as I think I'm in control (Marshall, 1992). But how do I better learn to maneuver through these understandings of language (and silence), these collections of memories? Why did I choose these stories in particular? What stories am I not telling, even not remembering?

And why *was* I silent/silenced at the meeting? Because of the often negative (if not indifferent) way "Women in Medicine" is perceived by so many at our institution? Because I was unable to access these particular men's understandings, that is, their scripted response to our presence in that room and our intended presence in their hospitals? Because I was afraid to break the social contract of behavior expected in that room? (I doubt my public display that afternoon was anything remarkable, or that anyone present knew how intensely felt the experience was for me.) Because of a "deeply felt rage at those who live their unexamined privilege as entitlement" (Lewis, 1993, p. 3) and my inability to articulate that rage? All are undoubtedly factors (plus some others that remain unknown to me), but the rage seems to be the most distinct. Yet, as I write these sentences now, I still feel as though I am telling a naughty story or breaking a code of discretion, thereby risking the security and protection of those who think me too nice, too much the team player to write this in so public a forum.

So, I tell this story. After writing it, however, I read it back and find no new truths and offer no guidance here to others engaged in similar struggles. So what's the point? My intent is to put this forth as a private struggle over meaning, but it is a struggle that is not devoid of political content. And because it is not, might it be potentially transformative? I think of writing from my experience as participating in what Jo Anne Pagano describes as a "discourse of affiliation" (1990, p. 11); such a discourse challenges and may weaken the cultural and institutional powers that have codified, vilified, or ignored women's lives. And finally, as Pearl Cleage puts it,

> I am writing to try and communicate . . . information to my sisters first and
> then to any brothers of goodwill and honest intent who will take the time to
> listen. . . . I am writing to allow myself to feel the anger. I am writing to keep
> from running toward it or away from it or into anybody's arms. . . . I am
> writing to find a language and pass it on. I am writing, writing, writing, for
> my life. (1993, p. 7)

———————

Autobiography is a vital current in feminist theorizing. With that as a
given, questions still remain as I try to transform my experiential belong-
ings into words on the page without telling readers what I think they
should know because they've read my stories. Do my stories tell readers
what they already know? Or, implicit in the concreteness of my stories,
intertwined with others' stories, do readers find different ways to think
about our overlapping concerns? Madeline Grumet reminds us that multiple stories, of which mine is a part, help "splinter the dogmatism of a
single tale" (quoted in Pinar, Reynolds, Slattery, & Taubman, 1995, p. 546),
and disturb any tendencies toward ahistorical, essentialist accountings of
women's experience.

Moreover, it seems to me that writers in the service of social change
must recognize reading as a process of discovery and must remember the
materiality of language that "resists the implied separation of form and
content" (Wicomb, 1991, pp. 14–15). The form and content of personal
theorizing is, of course, inseparable, but how can I presume to be a
scholar concerned with social change who doesn't consider the readers I
want to reach? Gayle Greene (1993) suggests that there are more people,
both inside and outside the academy, who just might read our work if we
spoke more directly to their lives, and if the ideas we presented were
useful. She urges

> that we stop dancing attendance on those who still have the power to confer
> rewards and benefits (and there are endless versions of this insidious game),
> that we envision our audience not as that patriarch in our head who may
> finally confer approval on us, but think of ourselves, rather, as reaching
> people to whom we have a responsibility . . . whether or not they can do us
> any good. (p. 20)

Yet merely telling stories, doing autobiographical "theorizing," and
being an "academic for social change" do not necessarily avoid the exclusionary tactics found in the primping, swaggering, and flaunting of abstract, inaccessible scholarship. Indeed, the ambiguity so often touted as
being one of the many virtues of abstruse writing (from the "complex

ideas require complex language" camp)—the kind of writing that often leaves readers bewildered and feeling stupid and poorly read—is not the ambiguity of narratives that provide readers with personal openings in received knowledge and the taken for granted. Put forth as part of a discourse of affiliation, these narratives "draw our life worlds out of obscurity so we may bring our experience to the patriarchal descriptions that constitute our sense of what it means to know, to nurture, to think, to succeed" (Grumet, 1988, p. 61).

So where does language "work," especially in the service of social change? Where are the moments when we come together not in fearful silence and not reciting chants, slogans, and scripts of our politics and our professions? Where words, with all their deceptions and contradictions, take us beyond ourselves for a moment, now or later, to reflect self-consciously and self-critically on the way we live our lives, to move us to work toward social change?

I hurriedly walk into my 8:00 A.M. literature and medicine class, arms full of books, slightly breathless, leaving a trail of coffee on the floor. There they are, the objects of my respect, often affection, and frustration: fourth-year medical students. Clutching their own huge mugs of coffee from McDonalds, these young doctors are talking quietly among themselves, usually on the most important issues in their lives: their upcoming residencies, apartment hunting, car buying, weddings. They are on the cusp of life, medical school being only preparation for it. They are in my class because (1) it fits well in their schedule, (2) they have missed fiction during their training and are happy to have this respite for reading literature, or (3) they just want the credit. I like them enormously. I look at them often and wonder how anything can be amiss in medicine.

My goals for this class, for all of my teaching, are to move us toward impatience with what Maxine Greene (1994) calls the "monological, the univocal way of making sense," and to pose

> questions involving what constitutes knowledge, what validates knowledge claims, how "truth" is to be defined, how social and cultural conditions affect scientific investigations, how "understanding" differs from "knowledge," what "meaning" signifies, and what belief systems and locations in the world have to do with the determination of what is taken to be "real" and "true." (p. 425)

Moreover, I want to encourage students to move from their pre-self-reflective mode of biochemistry and Krebs cycles and persons-as-patients to a mode of reflective praxis: to see needs, injustices, and omissions; to feel compelled to act upon them and against them; to imagine stand-points other than their received, medicalized realities; to look hard at the ways they dominate and oppress even as they devote their lives to healing.

I look for an empty seat at the conference center. I find one next to Ed, a striking, very intelligent young man, Korean-American, who has been accused of incredible arrogance by one of my women colleagues but whom I find a delight. He challenges me, his classmates, and the text often, and he sometimes does get a bit patronizing, but I am always struck by his reflectiveness and vulnerability. Because he's going into obstetrics/ gynecology, today Ed could be a real bugger because of what we are about to discuss.

We will be examining Lynne Sharon Schwartz's (1987) "So You're Going to Have a New Body," a deeply cynical, confrontive, angry story written as the inner dialogue of a woman who has just had a hysterec-tomy. This is not a good time in students' training to critique medicine the way this story does: They are full of themselves, their profession, and its status. They have worked hard, often at great emotional and financial expense, for the privilege of writing MD after their names, which they will be doing for the first time in a few weeks. Nonetheless, we take the plunge.

Schwartz's narrator, whose name is never disclosed, relates the fol-lowing chronology of her hysterectomy: mild pressure by her gynecolo-gist for removal of her ovaries at the time of surgery; an uneven recovery with unexpected physical and emotional responses; her unconventional healing, with residual ill feelings toward her doctor in particular, gyne-cologists in general.

Not surprisingly, students identify more with the gynecologist, who is seemingly competent but somewhat oblivious to emotions, than with the patient. They are impatient, even annoyed with her. Stephanie, Jay, and Rich say she is "whiny." Ed is exasperated with her because she takes no responsibility for initiating questions about her surgery and its effects on her body. Josh, Penny, and Suresh are irritated because of the hostility in her fantasies of how she will somehow turn the tables on her gynecolo-gist in a twisted reverse pelvic exam. Harriet and Nerraj do acknowledge how difficult a hysterectomy is for many women but believe her actions and emotional reactions go well beyond a "normal" response.

What does "whiny" mean, I ask, and what does the narrator do that invokes this label? Students cite her "oversensitivity" to ordinary occur-rences—her daughter's menstrual cramps, a Mary Cassatt jigsaw puzzle of a mother and daughter, her doctor's receptionist calling her "honey"—

none of which are worthy of such cynical ruminations, they say. But what does it mean to be *too* sensitive, I ask, and who sets the standards? Where does gender fit in here? Some squirming at this point: Several students do not want to say what they think—that some women patients *do* whine. Male patients may be difficult, or noncompliant, or "act like babies," but they *do not whine*.

Ed's problem is not with her attitude, exactly. His impatience is because she just sits there, right there in front of the doctor, full of questions and concerns, and won't say anything, even as she blames him for not anticipating everything she wants to know. She has no right to get on his case, he says. She is obviously an articulate, well-educated, and assertive patient, so there is no reason for her to pout and simmer silently because he is not providing the "right" information.

We explore this together for some time. Students' responses range from vehement disagreement with the whole notion of differential treatment based on gender ("it doesn't happen") to acknowledgment that it does indeed happen (and defending it). I ask if there is anything in the doctor–patient relationship even without the overlay of gender that prevents the kind of patient assertiveness Ed expects. This moves discussion into issues of power and authority, and the status of physician-as-secular-priest in contemporary U.S. culture. We puzzle over how this came to pass; suggest differences in patients' behaviors and expectations according to age, class, and gender; think about physicians' relational responsibilities in light of these differences.

I pause and look around the room and think how satisfying this is for me. Students are really thinking here, I tell myself. No, that is not quite right. Maybe this: I believe students are trying very hard here to reflect on the taken-for-granted in medicine that their training (indeed, their culture) has instilled in them. I hope this reflectiveness reappears beyond these moments in the classroom—at the bedside, taking a history, talking to the family. That is, I hope this sharing of thoughts and experiences in the classroom is part of a social praxis "that entails reflection and political action" (Freire & Macedo, 1995, p. 380).

For me the classroom, *this* classroom, is one of those elusive places beyond silences and scripts. Not always, of course, but every now and then—without warning or planning—it happens: We talk to each other, reflect out loud and silently, relax our respective postures, critique our thinking, see things as they might be. We do it with words, those slippery, wily constructions that make us human.

Yet sometimes I wonder if I am fooling myself. My perception of what goes on in my classes is always mediated through the screens of

my beliefs and hopes for this whole teaching/learning enterprise. I recall
Deanne Bogdan's thinking about her classes, especially when she asks,

> How do I know that what looks like everyone riding our communal bicycle
> is not really a coercive regime masking silences and erasing hostilities? And
> conversely, given that my role is so fraught with paradox, especially in a
> feminist class, where I am invariably cast as "the bearded mother" (expected
> to be both supportive emotionally and rigorous scholastically), how do I
> know that something quite wonderful is not happening to someone? (1994,
> p. 351)

I am just beginning to accept that I cannot (should not) divest myself
of my authority, that I have spent too many years invoking "a romantic
pedagogic mode that exoticizes discussing lived experiences as a process
of coming to voice" (Freire & Macedo, p. 381). Indeed, I confused dialogue as conversation and technique, rather than as an epistemological
relationship between myself and my students that recognizes "the social
and not merely the individualistic characteristic of the process of knowing" (p. 379). In the former, dialogue is reduced to a "vacuous feel good
comfort zone"; in the latter, it is "a process of learning and knowing [that]
must always involve a political project with the objective of dismantling
oppressive structures and mechanisms prevalent in . . . society" (p. 380).

I no longer presume to "work across differences" in classrooms
where students (well-intentioned, empathic, each caught in multiple cultural nets) have come of age in the era of Reagan–Bush, Rush Limbaugh,
and notions of "family values" that exclude most of the world, and certainly most oppressed groups. Feminist and antiracist/anticlassist trans-
formations *are* explicit goals in my classes; thus the thinking of even the
(seemingly) most caring and skilled medical students who call health
care a privilege and AIDS God's wrath becomes a major problem for me.
I believe such students are often unaware of the effects of their thinking
on their doctoring even as they vehemently insist that they give "equal"
treatment to all regardless of their patients' ability to pay or physical
appearance.

I think of the day we read Irvin Yalom's (1989) story, "Fat Lady." That
day talk was difficult, with frequent silences, moments of awkward
squirming, and eyes avoiding contact. These are more likely to occur
when the issue we're examining goes beneath the protection of their new
white coats—that is, when I ask students to confront their (our) racism
and sexism, or their biases against poor people, gays and lesbians, or
obese people.

Yalom's confessional story is painful to read. We are embarrassed for
the narrator—a psychiatrist—who tells readers about his disgust with

obesity, particularly in women. He knows that he is not alone in his prejudice, that cultural reinforcement is everywhere ("who ever has a kind
word for the fat lady?"), but his contempt exceeds all cultural norms—
never mind the misogyny of the norms themselves. So when Betty, a 250-
pound, 5'2" woman comes into his office for treatment of her eating disorder, he knows his bias will get in the way of the therapy she seeks.

The story unfolds, then, as the narrator and his patient struggle
together for over a year, the latter with her psychological "emptiness,"
her isolation, her hunger for closeness; the former with, as he describes
it ". . . er . . . [my] problem with obesity" (p. 115). Betty becomes aware of
and even changes many habits that had led her to her current physical
state, and the narrator moves from being unable to make eye contact to
being more fully present to Betty during their sessions ("I no longer no-
ticed her body and, instead, looked into her eyes"), to feeling outrage
and empathy for her daily despair at the mockery she receives as a fat
woman, to their final session when he writes, "I didn't want to stop seeing
Betty. I wanted to keep on talking to her, to keep on knowing her" (p. 117).

"Fat Lady" can work in a number of potentially transformative ways.
First, reading it can provide a way for students to recognize their biases;
second, the discourse surrounding the reading can help students begin
the hard work of challenging biases as the narrator of "Fat Lady" does,
to begin to uncover how the nature of the care they give to others can be
significantly influenced by these very biases. For the essential first step
of Dr. Yalom's journey to acceptance of his patient was his willingness to
confront his prejudice rather than pretend that it did not exist or that it
would not prevent keep him from skillfully doing his job. The courage
he displayed in his unflinchingly honest examination of his bias may give
students license to self-critique more honestly, less afraid of the ugly or
"unacceptable" feelings they may find there. And then they might begin
the lifelong unlearning of beliefs that devalue other humans.

Yet, as it came to me later, we had inadvertently valorized the narrator in this story. Everything seemed so successful and tidy at story's
end: Yalom's narrator was working toward confronting his bias against
fat women, and Betty had lost weight. Somewhere in the midst of all this,
the doctor became the hero, and Betty became the vehicle for him to work
through his problems. Indeed, chatty as Betty had been as a patient (one
of the many ways she masked her pain, said her doctor), she was shad-
owed—visually silenced—at the end by the shining light of the doctor's
"success." His unexamined privilege as a doctor and transmitter of patriarchal medical and cultural norms never really entered his self-scrutiny;
the fact that he recognized a bias and disclosed it never touched the issue
of the pathologized female body. That is, his scripted "take" on the self-

reflective physician who dares to uncover personal biases is seductive enough to help readers forget that the rules of what constitute health and healing remain largely unexamined.

My role? I find myself somewhere between urges for didactic, staged classroom performances intended to "correct" students' ideologies that dominate and oppress—my scripts—and the problematic relativism of respecting and providing space for *all* opposing viewpoints—my silences, which "merely orchestrate the participation of students in pure verbalism" (Freire & Macedo, p. 383). Such pluralism that does little more than acknowledge differences neglects the significance of the challenge and thus ignores power imbalances in the class, in the stories we read, in the world outside.

I do, however, tell students that I do not believe I have a lock on the Truth; I do not believe I have found a coherent narrative to explain the world or form a perfect one; I do not believe I am exempt from assuming the oppressor role, and I acknowledge my own implication in knowledge production. Even as I write this narrative I recognize, like many other feminists, that when we "draw on cultural traditions that have been eclipsed by the pretensions of the most powerful, [we] are always in danger of relapsing into claims of privileged access, of reproducing the cultural arrogance [we] seek to undermine" (R. B. J. Walker, 1988, p. 151).

Still, I do believe that when I tentatively remove my finger from the dike of my own constructed world, fearful of what may come rushing (or trickling) through, uncertain of how the landscape may be changed, I can facilitate the kind of communication across differences (I am still not sure how inclusive "difference" can be) that Elizabeth Ellsworth writes about: toward understanding that all our understandings/knowledge of each other, the world, and "the Right thing to do"—a daily question in medicine—will always be partial, interested, and potentially oppressive to others (Ellsworth, 1989).

But is that enough? To move students to recognize the complexities of knowledge, language, power, and perception; to confront how difficult it is *not* to make presumptions, to dishonor and suppress others; to begin to think about how they might work for social change? For here, for the time being, until I figure out more: You bet that's enough.

———

Because the story of our life
becomes our life

Because each of us tells
the same story
but tells it differently

> and none of us tells it
> the same way twice
>
> . . . .
>
> and though we listen only
> haphazardly, with one ear,
> we will begin our story
> with the word and
> —Lisel Mueller,
>   "Why We Tell Stories"

I just told three stories from my own experience—at leisure, during a meeting, and in a classroom, stories from my life imbued with silence, anger, hesitation, joy, doubt, and hope. As I sifted through my experiences, I searched for stories that would resonate with readers, to make this that I call my research—what marks me as a scholar in the academy—embody what Bakhtin defined in the novel as a "multiplicity of styles," to echo with others "as the word constantly reinvolved in a dialogue" (Pomorska, 1984, p. ix). I am in dialogue with readers, here and long after I finish; with others' words in text and talk; and always, deeply with myself.

This fluid, untamable dialogic life is not programmed to begin when I arrive at my office and turn on my computer. The stories of our lives, which *are* our lives, are intertwined with the details and conditions of our living, who and what we love, what we call work and pleasure, what we read and watch and hear, how we treat one another and the way we are treated—and more. The stuff of my theorizing, then, is made up of many ingredients, not just using others' thinking to read mine. It occurs on the phone talking to my sister; in a restroom exchange with a colleague or at the faculty table in the cafeteria; in heated discussion after seeing a film with students.

How much more can I say about my stories?

I do not believe the act of storytelling (or the stories themselves) is based on the assumption of a singular, fixed, essential self. I tell and read stories of personal experience "within and against the many other fictions of the world around us" (Gough, 1995, p. 7). As such, I am searching for ways to use language that are seamless: where there is no back-and-forth between ideas and emotion, personal and academic, creative and critical; where telling stories and talking about those stories can be the same; where writing for others is writing for ourselves. I am finding new understandings that the way I write is intertwined with the way I teach, and both, of course, are inseparable from the I who lives in those hours outside the academy.

So I keep on writing, using the father tongue, yes, but trying to change the rules for its use; language fails even when it succeeds. For now, like Nancy Mairs,

> don't ask me for impregnable argument. As far as I'm concerned, my text is flawed not when it is ambiguous or even contradictory, but only when it leaves you no room for stories of your own. I keep my tale as wide open as I can. (1994, p. 76)

Thus, I not only begin my story with the word *and*, I should like to end it that way too.

3

Breaking the Ice in Thawing Climates: Feminism in Medical Education

On the name of the Women and Medicine program: "I think it should be an ombudsman office, or an office of gender studies, or something that doesn't focus exclusively on women."

On my literature and medicine syllabus, particularly the section on women's health issues in literature: "Why isn't there a section on men's health issues?"

As a feminist in a medical academy for over a decade, I am still and always surprised not only at the relative lack of a feminist presence in that institution but also at the scornful associations with the word itself. I wonder how and why medical education has remained seemingly immune from a broad-based feminist critique from within, given the fervent intellectual feminist debate in college and university settings and in the larger U.S. culture. I look at the energy, ambition, and intelligence of women students and colleagues who often face the difficulties of blending demanding careers with other full-time responsibilities of partners, children, and extended families and friends, not to mention other interests outside medicine. I see these same women year after year, *not* moving in appropriate numbers into positions of increasing authority and prestige in the academic ranks and clinical specialties. I know, and they know, that medical education—indeed the huge and powerful social institution of U.S. medicine—is controlled by a huge majority of white men. Yet as I look at these same extraordinary women, I am aware that not many would name themselves feminist.

In this chapter I will describe several feminist projects that have been undertaken in academic medicine and explore how a larger systemic feminist effort might look and proceed in that setting. But first, I attempt an ecumenical definition of *feminism* not only to establish my position here but to work toward inclusiveness in the larger political project to improve women's lives.

This, of course, is tricky. "A" definition of feminism does not exist even within academic feminist theorizing, even though most people have an opinion on its meaning and those who espouse it, due in no small part to living in a patriarchal culture and being exposed to media that often caricature feminists. Yet the very rich diversity within this political movement includes (but is not limited to) liberal feminism, materialist feminism, and postmodern feminism; there is Anglo-American feminism and Continental feminism; there are Western and non-Western feminists; there are variations in these and more. Moreover, feminism is fueled by the overlapping yet unique concerns of women of color, working-class women, lesbians and heterosexual women, older women, and disabled women. Which is why at this historical moment some feminist theorists have attempted to erase the analytic category "woman" even as we hear urgings for a "new," previously dismissed category "women" in biomedical research, a category that heretofore didn't even exist in many clinical trials with exclusively male subjects (generalized, nonetheless, to all women).

Indeed, most feminist theorizing suggests that it is impossible to speak of "woman" without also noting her socioeconomic status, her race, her sexual orientation, and where she calls home in the larger world. Those who do not make such distinctions, who continue to speak of "woman" as a universal category, are charged with essentialism, an error in thought that ascribes innate qualities to a group based on biology, race, ethnicity, or other common characteristics, and that is quite a serious intellectual failing. Taken to its extreme, essentialism is likely to strangle the breadth and depth of human differences within such groups, keeping women and other Others in subordinate positions as their universal "characteristics" are inevitably compared to white, male norms. (See Chapter 6 for additional discussion of essentialism.)

This is not to say that even in the absence of a universal category "woman" there can be no feminism. Quite the contrary—at least one common goal links women all over the world across our differences and internal debates: to end the subordination of women and other oppressed people. Susan Sherwin (1992b) writes of this inevitably political dimension of feminist theory,

> that women are in a subordinate position in society, that oppression is a form of injustice and hence is intolerable, that there are further forms of oppression in addition to gender oppression (and that there are women victimized by each of these forms of oppression), that it is possible to change society in

ways that could eliminate oppression, and that it is a goal of feminism to pursue the changes necessary to accomplish this. (p. 29)

How would this broadly based feminist critique be received in medical education? Up to this point, most feminist debate has been framed to keep women on the defensive, working *within* the existing educational framework by "offering hope for improvement—but only if they did not rock the patriarchal boat too vigorously" (Warren, 1992, p. 34). Working within a prescribed arena keeps debate surrounding gender fairness away from the larger foundational critique of an institution—here, the medical academy—that continues to operate on an unequal power relationship between women and men (Sherwin, 1992a). Still, feminist efforts within that arena have made important headway in improving the quality of life for women in academic medicine, efforts I will discuss below.

Within the confines of this chapter, I emphatically recognize wide variability among women even as I acknowledge a fluid, socially constructed category "woman." I "take the risk" of essentialism here and throughout these pages in order to work collectively toward gender fairness and other issues of equity in medical education. Thus, in my effort to define feminism, I turn to Sherwin's attempt to connect the various feminisms with one another even as I resist a totalizing theoretical position. Critical to her (and my) analysis of medicine and medical education

are the understandings that women are oppressed, that this oppression is pervasive in all aspects of social life, and that political action (that is, collective action on a broad scale) is necessary to understand and eliminate that oppression from our world. . . . [Moreover], the practice of medicine serves as an important instrument in the continuing disempowerment of women (and members of other oppressed groups) in society. (1992a, p. 32; 1992b, p. 22)

FEMINISM IN THE MEDICAL ACADEMY:
(SOME) CURRENT INDICATORS

With Sherwin's definition loosely in place and with the disclaimer that I do not attempt to speak for all women in academic medicine, I have selected two problematic areas in the lives of women in medical education. I will discuss how these problems have been confronted, suggest additional ways to address them, and propose a more systemic feminist critique of academic medicine.

Sexual Harassment

First, a common language. Sexual harassment is a form of gender discrimination that can lead to legal action. It comes in many forms that can be divided into two basic types: the *quid pro quo,* or *bargain,* variety (the "I'll flunk you if you don't have sex with me" scenario) and the *hostile environment* variety. *Gender discrimination,* the larger term under which *sexual harassment* falls, describes the actions, practices, and other policies that negatively affect women because of different treatment or impact they receive, or the creation of a hostile work environment. Some particularly ugly kinds of gender discrimination have legal implications; some forms, however repulsive, do not. These include language that deprecates women, treatment of women as unseen, negative attitudes of women's ability based on gender, and deletion of women from informal networks. Multiple enactments of these microinequities can contribute to a hostile environment. Medical students encounter these kinds of negative gender-related incidents most frequently (Nora, 1996).

Sexual harassment in medical training has been well documented throughout the United States. Lenhart, Klein, Falcao, Phelan, and Smith (1991) found that 54% of the women physicians and medical students surveyed encountered some form of sex discrimination during a one-year period. Komaromy, Bindman, Haber, and Sande (1993) asked medicine residents at the University of California, San Francisco, if they had experienced sexual harassment during medical school and residency; they found that nearly three-quarters of the female residents said they had been sexually harassed, in many cases more than once. Ehrhart and Sandler (1990) reported that in one study at the University of Wisconsin School of Medicine, 33% of the women surveyed said they had experienced sexual harassment from a person in a position of authority. Baldwin, Daugherty, and Eckenfels (1991) made the following distinctions in their survey at ten medical schools: 28.9% of the women respondents experienced sexual advances; 61.5% experienced sexist slurs ("honey," "dollface," "sweetie," etc.); and 25.7% reported sexist teaching materials used in their training.

What do these studies tell us? That harassed students pay a heavy toll: Sexual harassment interferes with their ability to concentrate, study, and work in the environment where it happens; they circumvent training opportunities because of past episodes of harassing behavior; their performance drops; their selection of a residency program may be affected (Nora, 1996, p. 115).

What else do these studies tell us? That over and above the ubiquitous gender discrimination found in most institutions, the more flagrant

forms of sexual harassment are remarkably widespread even in the prestigious profession of medicine, a profession dedicated to the care of human bodies and spirits, a profession dedicated to health-*seeking* behaviors. These studies tell us that leering, sexual innuendos and comments,
jokes about sex or women in general, unwanted touching or other physical contact, and subtle or direct suggestions or threats for sex can thwart,
diminish, or crush the spirit, confidence, and ambition of women at any
age or level of professional attainment.

Ehrhart and Sandler (1990) describe the potential effects of verbal or
physical harassment *regardless of the intentions of the harasser:*

> It . . . may make women feel like outsiders—their sexuality becomes more
> important than their intellectual ability and medical skills. Moreover, sexual
> harassment can damage a woman's self-esteem and her growth as a person
> who feels herself equal to men and able to work with them. The tension it
> creates also can distract a woman from the tasks she has to perform. . . . A
> woman can spend a good deal of emotional energy trying to figure out what
> she ought to do, how to handle her anger, and in the case of more subtle
> behaviors, wondering whether she even has cause to be uncomfortable. (p. 7)

Wondering whether she even has cause to be uncomfortable. Such self-doubt
goes to the heart of the ancient oppression of women, when even in the
face of slurs, suggestions, threats, and coercion, she asks: "Did *I* do anything to provoke this behavior?"

Of course, many medical schools have confronted the problem of
sexual harassment by providing stern policies of what constitutes harassment, what procedural guidelines are encouraged if not mandated, what
the consequences are for harassers, and what will be done to protect the
victim of harassment (Gordon, Labby, & Levinson, 1992; Lenhart, Klein,
Falcao, Phelan, & Smith, 1991; Riger, 1991). These efforts are critical. Yet,
like the continuing legacy of racism in the United States, we all know
that legislation cannot begin to dismantle thousands of years of patriarchic and sometimes misogynist practices, any more than legislation un-
raveled the complexities, insidiousness, and sometimes unconsciousness
of racial oppression.

What to do with all this is particularly difficult because most episodes of abuse in medical training go unreported (Baldwin et al., 1991;
Farley & Kozarsky, 1993; Grant, 1988; Komaromy et al., 1993). Because of
this huge gap between frequency and actual cases reported, relying on
litigation may not be the best approach. Sexual harassment must be identified and confronted from its most seemingly innocuous forms to the
ugliness of pressure, bribes, or threats for sex. Once policies are in place,
noisy and public enforcement must be the rule; denial, impression man-

agement, and confusing confidentiality with secrecy must be openly confronted.

Moreover, *theorizing* sexual harassment needs to be more thorough: Merely attributing it to power—clearly obvious—and moving on to verbal and behavioral indicators and procedural guidelines leaves foundational questions unanswered. How is sexual harassment tied to the larger imbalance of power in university settings? How is sexual harassment in medical training additionally tied to power imbalances in the rigidly gendered medical profession? Carr (1991) theorizes that the university is an oasis for persons addicted to power and uses an addiction framework to explain and describe how power addicts sexually harass. What is the medical overlay to this theory of addiction to power? What is the effect of multiple Band-Aids on an institution built on and continuously infused with and reproducing authority, control, hierarchies, rigid turf rules, and deference to specialization?

Of course, we can theorize all the way to the most highly regarded journals and conference proceedings, but such abstracted efforts will just not work at the local level for which they are intended without local leadership. This is not to ignore the fact that deeply committed women (and men who act on their verbal commitment to this matter) have brought about enormous changes in medicine, often in indifferent if not hostile environments. Yet as Frances Conley (1993) persuasively argues, it is

> the top echelon at any academic institution that sets the tone for its workplace and educational environment. A sexist or racist cast at the top translates into a validation of sexual harassment or racial hatred as an acceptable form of behavior among the membership and guarantees its perpetuation into the next generation. . . . In those we choose to guide us, technical talent and academic credentials must be coupled with decent behavior. (p. 352)

Decent behavior. How deceptively simple, yet how complicated and historicized a goal it is.

Representation and Professional Development

After a recent meeting of a dozen or so people that included faculty and administrators, we were discussing the huge numbers of women entering the profession and the increase (albeit very, very slow) in the number of women in traditionally male fields such as orthopedics and general surgery. The conversation shifted to the topic of affirmative action, and not surprisingly this group of white, middle-class, middle-aged men, all of them comfortable and accomplished, questioned the need for its existence. I am incredulous, impatient, and angry in these conversations, unable to grasp a position that perceives the medical environment as gender-fair (or oblivious to color), and was reminded of Faye Crosby's wry paper title: "Sex Discrimination: How Can We Correct It if We Can't See It? And How Can We See It if We're Not Prepared to Correct It?" (quoted in Walsh, 1990, p. 302).

Numbers tell part of the story. For the last three years, an equal proportion of women and men have been accepted at U.S. medical schools. In the 1994–95 academic year, women made up the majority of new entrants at 18 medical schools; new entrants who are women range from 25% to 56% across U.S. medical schools. The percentage of women in residency programs has grown from 22% in 1980 to 33% of all residents in 1994. The number of full-time faculty who are women has increased from 15% in 1975 to 25% in 1995 (Bickel et al., 1995). But numbers do not tell all; in fact, as Pressman (1991) reminds us, "the numbers do not add up to equality" (p. 44). In spite of these increasing figures, women are *not* making significant gains at levels of power and authority, most notably in the offices of deans, department chairs, and other significant positions (see Chapter 1).

With all these numbers in mind, it is not surprising that many women perceive medical institutions to be both covertly and explicitly sexist. Hostler and Gressard (1993) reported a recent survey at the University of Virginia School of Medicine that measured student, house staff, and faculty perceptions of the gender fairness of their medical education environment. The survey also examined the effects of gender and academic group status on these perceptions and elicited suggestions for improving the status of women in terms of compensation, professional development, and representation. A score of *less* than 42 indicated a perception of the existence of sexism and inequity; a score of *more* than 42 indicated a perception that sexism and inequity did not exist. The following results were reported: Women generally did not perceive the medical education environment as gender-fair, with mean scores ranging from 34.2 (faculty) to 37.8 (students); men generally did not perceive a lack of gender fairness, with mean scores ranging from 46.88 (faculty) to 44.63 (students).

What is currently being done in situations like this, who is doing it, and what additional measures should be taken? The excuse that it will "just take time" for women to move into positions of power and authority, that it will just "naturally" occur over time, no longer works. Women have been in medicine long enough to see their presence at all levels, in all specialties. The reasons for their absence in these places are complicated, with some being the result of overt sexism while others are more subtle. No matter what the causes of these patterns, what remains is that when women are sorted into niches compatible with traditional women's roles, "gender equality is diminished and the significance of women's increasing access to medicine is minimized. . . . A key issue is the extent to which women control their own career choices within medicine" (A. P. Williams, Pierre, & Vayda, 1993, p. 119).

Power and authority usually are not cheerfully given by those who hold it to those who have been denied it; women must work actively, openly, and unapologetically to end sexist practices in academic medicine. One overwhelming task here is to recruit more women faculty to be leaders, mentors, and role models for students, residents, and other faculty. Zealous networking must be established and maintained to put out the word when positions open for department chairs, assistant and associate deans, and yes, deans. Women must relentlessly apply for these positions in increasing numbers. Women must insist that an appropriate number of women serve on search committees for these positions. Women must, even in the face of their overstuffed, overcommitted lives, mentor young women, steadily encouraging them to examine *all* specialty and administrative options. Yet, to avoid perpetuating the unattainable, unhealthy mythology of superwoman–doctor, women must invent new strategies that do not make a full family life—however one defines *family*—and a vibrant professional life mutually exclusive. Given that many women will have children during their training, medical schools and hospitals must, as another form of fair and decent behavior, develop policies that make sure pregnant women (and their peers) are treated fairly. Similarly, academic medicine must develop strategies such as "stop-the-clock" programs that permit parents who are raising children to add a year or more to the tenure timetable.

Now I leave the Band-Aid approaches to "fixing" sexism in academic medicine—essential as they are—and move into broader, systemic, foundational issues that must also be addressed. While my intent here is clearly not to medicine-bash—I am a privileged beneficiary of the world's finest system of medical care, and a patient of skilled and caring physicians—I believe that some aspects of academic medicine require critical scrutiny and change. Thus, while my language may seem excessively critical, I use it to evoke the kind of personal and institutional scrutiny so important to this kind of inquiry.

FEMINISM IN THE MEDICAL ACADEMY: NEW AND LARGER WAVES

Feminist ethicists have taken medical institutions to task for their complicity in some aspects of the oppression of women. Sherwin (1992a) summarizes this complicity:

The institution of medicine has been designed in ways that reinforce sexism, and the effects of medical practice are often bad for women. Most individual medical actions make sense in the context of medicine as it is currently defined, but we need to step back and examine the cumulative effects of some of its practices. We need to see the patterns of medical values and structures as a whole, in order to identify some of the connections between medical practice and patriarchy; only then can we see the sorts of changes that should be made. As long as we focus on the merely personal—that is, on an individual encounter with a particular doctor—we cannot see the systematic force of sexist assumptions in our health care institutions. (p. 6)

Where does all this start? It begins in a system of medical training that boasts some of the most profound socialization found in any profession, a socialization that "often forces those in training to absorb the values of the dominant group" and that leads to some of the fiercest loyalty to a profession by its members. Indeed, gender differences are actually diminished as students wind through the "intense and homogenizing effects of professional socialization" (Walsh, 1990, p. 302). From the first days of training, medical students find themselves in a rigid hierarchy, a caste system of power and authority with the physician at the top (and, as we have seen, those particular physicians are almost all men) and medical students near the bottom. Only those most directly responsible for patients' physical care—overwhelmingly women, that is, the RNs, the LPNs, the aides, and so on—are at the bottom of the heap in terms of professional authority, prestige, and financial rewards.

Yet, as neurosurgeon Frances Conley (1993) reminds us, in spite of this sorting game, medicine has never been able to function without women's labors. She recounts that after reading David Noonan's bestselling book *Neuro-*, she asked:

Where were the women? Where were the ones on the wards and intensive care units, drawing blood, taking x-ray films, handing instruments, cleaning a bloody operating room after the triumphal exit of the neurosurgeon hero? . . . the women became, yet again, nearly invisible. We all live with a social concept, tacitly accepted by both men and women, that in the medical profession, men are dominant and women subservient. (p. 352)

Medical students absorb all this quickly, adding it to their already full purse of culturally induced, implicit, often unexamined sexist beliefs.

Students also quickly learn that the epistemology of medicine values and rewards certain knowledge while devaluing or at least ascribing lesser status to other knowledge. Dualisms become firmly entrenched: objective/subjective, reason/emotion, distance/connection, abstract/particular (the former in each dyad being that which is most valued).

Collaboration and nonhierarchical relationships between and among health care professionals, doctors, and patients based on authentic mutuality and collegiality—components of much feminist theorizing—may be espoused theoretically in medical training but may be difficult to see practiced in hospital settings where norms have been established and are rigidly maintained.

Similarly, a work life that significantly interweaves family, social, and community life, so that one's identity is not bound into a model of doctor-as-all-consuming-hero, may be hard for young women in training to find, especially if they aspire to specialties dominated by men. Women continue to question how they can have a full and meaningful family life *and* a satisfying, fulfilling career—concerns I have rarely seen male medical students ponder in all my years as a medical educator. Yet such questions are understandable for many women to ask within the context of patriarchal structures of work and definitions of what constitutes a successful medical career; such questions are almost unavoidable for women.

Still, discussion of these issues in training may be myopic, failing to take into account the larger foundational aspects of medical training. That is, the institution is usually accepted as a *given*, while debates (such as the ones raised here) have, according to Sherwin (1992b), "focused on certain practices within that structure. . . . The effect is to provide an ethical legitimization of the institution overall, with acceptance of its general structures and patterns" (pp. 22–23). Writing specifically about medical ethics (yet relevant to this discussion), Sherwin charges that feminists have remained largely silent about the medical practices that contribute directly to the oppression of women. The "deep questions about the structure of medical practice and its role in a patriarchal society" remain largely unasked on this level (p. 23).

What are we to do? I return to my initial musings about the seeming lack of an explicit feminist presence in medical education. I cautioned then, as I do now, that I do not and cannot speak for all women in medicine, especially health care providers who are not physicians, or those characterized as "nonprofessional" in hospital settings. Moreover, women in medicine who are women of color, or lesbians, for example, face complexities unknown to me and other white, heterosexual women. Thus discussions of sexual harassment and career development may take new and more complicated turns for these and other women. Still, as I suggested earlier, I believe that there are forms of oppression we all face as women and that the political commitment of feminism to end gender inequity and hostility is, perhaps, one that medical women—students, residents, faculty—might consider with renewed vigor and commitment. As women collectively begin looking at the institution of medicine through feminist lenses, resisting the deeply encoded urge to "outman the men" that most mature women in active practice today had to enact, perhaps medical training can be reinvented.

Band-Aid efforts can and do promote piecemeal change. But sexual harassment, work and training sites that are deliberately hostile and intimidating to women, and positions of authority and prestige that systematically exclude women are all reflections of sexism on a grand scale in U.S. culture. As we focus on specific issues that detract from the quality of life for women in medicine, we must also develop a bifocal vision, looking up and around at the larger medical horizon, questioning its very structure and means of support. When we examine the bureaucracy of medical education, we might question its inherent nature, which rests on "rational division of labor, fixed job responsibilities, a system of supervision based on horizontal layers, rule-governed authority channels, elaborate systems for keeping written records, and so forth" (Johnson, 1993, p. 12); in our own departments and offices we can provide alternative ways to work together that are not based on power and control.

Moreover, we can turn a critical gaze on our *own* teaching, looking at how we interact with our students and the way we are with our colleagues and patients; we can observe the examples of our own professional and personal lives by decoding the overt and subtle messages we send to students, residents, and colleagues that reflect our real values and commitments. We can ask the hard questions (that many in primary care have been asking for some time) regarding what constitutes a successful medical career, one that may not rest on high levels of productivity and efficiency and that may not yield a large income (A. P. Williams et al., 1993, p. 119).

When we engage in such a critique, when we engage in reflective action on the world in order to change it, what we are doing is nothing less than the dailiness of a revolution. When women in medicine begin to name (or rename) themselves feminists and to act upon the commitments of feminism, this is to "change the way one lives in the world." This process, as Sherwin tells us, is "exciting, terrifying, exhilarating, confusing, challenging, depressing, frustrating, and joyous. . . . Once we learn to see how things really are, they are not easily hidden from us again" (1992a, p. 34). Living our feminist commitments as we educate young physicians to be technically skilled, caring, *and* respectful of the full range of human diversity in their patients and peers: What more could we ask for?

4

"What's Feminism Got to Do with It?" Medical Students' Perceptions of Feminism and Medicine

To acknowledge our ancestors means
we are aware that we did not make
ourselves, that the line stretches
all the way back
—Alice Walker,
"In These Dissenting Times"

Q: How do you define feminism?
A: (Jill, a first-year medical student): "Anti-everything . . . "

THIRD-GENERATION feminism. I wonder, is it possible? Does a new generation start before the one preceding it matures? Did second-generation feminism finish its work and I just have not recognized it yet? Or, I think of what Wendy Kaminer said: "We've managed to enter a postfeminist world without ever knowing a feminist one" (1990, p. 1).

Perhaps I have just not been listening. For years I have heard so many of my women students criticize if not eschew the very word *feminism* along with the women who espouse it. *Feminists:* a label they often use derisively and sarcastically, but even quizzically sometimes: "Who *are* these women?" they ask. Or: "Uh, excuse me . . . look around: Women do what men do in medicine . . . what's the deal here?" Well, of course, there are lots of women in my classes (nearing 50% these days), but, I ask my students, is the fact of higher numbers in the entry level of one of the most privileged of all professions cause to announce the death of a social movement focused on equity for *all* women? Maybe this is just medicine's particular take on feminism: Life is good for me; therefore the movement must have outlived its usefulness. Usually I dismiss their lack of interest in such issues as an indicator of age (young) and experience (a lack thereof). When they get older, I think, or when they live through this or that, they'll embrace feminism.

But first, a brief look back to see where third-generation feminists situate themselves historically and ideologically. There is some agreement that *first-generation* feminism in the United States was the late 19th- and early 20th-century movement for women's suffrage. *Second-generation* feminism began with the women's liberation movement of the 1960s and 1970s and extends into the present. It is concerned with issues surrounding gender equity in the workplace, such as day care and leave policies; reproductive freedom and other dimensions of women's health; legislative agendas such as the Equal Rights Amendment; antipornography campaigns, lesbian rights, and a general focus on oppression based on gender. Somewhere in the midst of all this, prompted by critiques from within and without, the feminist movement turned in on itself and found itself essentialist, elitist, and unwittingly racist. That it, the movement narrowly reflected the interests and agendas of white, educated, middle-class, mostly academic women and had thereby ignored the particular concerns of women of color, working-class or poor women, and non-Western women. Moreover, by erroneously attempting to speak for all women, feminism as an ideology implied that a universal category "woman" did indeed exist, thus sparking a debate that continues today on the subject of essentialism. As a result of this critique, feminists began to recognize that gender (and gender oppression) is not a unitary construct but rather part of a larger identity grid containing race, class, age, and sexual practice and that it is impossible to view any of these constructs as separate from the others. Thus today feminism—better yet, *feminisms*—are overlapping alliances of theoretical positions and political agendas, all circling back to women.

Now along comes *third-generation* feminism. We find Katie Roiphe's (1993) *The Morning After: Sex, Fear, and Feminism on Campus,* which acidly criticizes what she calls the feminist "preoccupation" with rape and sexual harassment that paints women into the corner of victimhood rather than fighting against it. Or Naomi Wolf's (1993) *Fire with Fire,* which similarly claims that the feminist emphasis on victimization estranges women, that women are fed up with hearing about oppression and are far more attracted by appeals to their strength, resourcefulness, and sense of responsibility. Camille Paglia (1992, 1994) fits in here, too, although I am not quite sure where, with her antifeminist performances.

More recently, Sherrye Henry (1994) and Rene Denfeld (1995) jumped on the backlash bandwagon by claiming that feminism does not speak to "mainstream" women, whoever they are. Like their successful sisters in the cottage industry that manufactures mass-produced critiques of the feminist movement, they find feminism (a monolith *they've* constructed) irrelevant, and both have ideas how to fix it: "Find out what's on the minds of ordinary American Women, adjust feminism accordingly, and *voilà*, gender inequalities will be solved once and for all" (Tanenbaum 1995, p. 5). One of the theses of Henry's book, *The Deep Divide: Why American Women Resist Equality,* is that American women should focus on our commonalities and that the movement (as if it exists out there independent of American women) should rid itself of activist types, those "hairy legs [that] haunt the feminist movement as do images of being strident and lesbian" (Wallis, quoted in Cowan, Mestlin, & Masek, 1992, p. 329). Moreover, Henry maintains, "no malevolent person or organized conspiracy holds women back from what is rightfully, constitutionally theirs. . . . Women voluntarily remain outside the Establishment's walls, unwilling to open the gates and walk in" (p. 2). Denfeld similarly charges in her book, *The New Victorians: A Young Woman's Challenge to the Old Feminist Order,* that after the ERA failed, the only things feminists could find to work on were "moral crusades against men, pornography, and sex. . . . The defeat also saw many mainstream women abandon the movement, leaving extremists to speak on behalf of feminism," claiming that "all sex is rape" and extolling the desirability of goddess worship and lesbian separatism (p. 17). In fact, Denfeld says, each notable feminist cause today estranges women.

None of this is new. Greene (1993) points out that feminism has already had one serious backlash during this century that occurred right after women won the vote. Indeed, *postfeminism* as a word to describe young women's disenchantment with feminism actually can be traced to 1919 when "a group of female literary radicals" who called their position postfeminist founded a new journal declaring an interest "in people . . . not in men and women" (Cott, quoted in G. Greene, 1993, p. 12).

Yet postfeminism is not merely a media gimmick, regardless of how happily feminists are bashed and parodied there. Backlash is everywhere, from the antifeminist beliefs of the young, to the tendency to blame feminism for the breakdown of the family—"it must be all that equality causing all that pain" (Faludi, 1991, p. x), to the appearance of new inequalities that now appear with the old ones, including the feminization of poverty, demonization of unmarried mothers, glass ceilings, brick walls, and sticky floors (Greene, 1993).

Now what does all this mean to medical students? First let me say that *of course* there are some students who proudly call themselves feminist. But I have found that if they[1] use the label at all, they (in third-generation spirit) heavily qualify it because of their impatience with "victim" feminism, one of the many perceived excesses of feminism as they see it. Many of them believe that although discrimination still does exist, our society is basically meritocratic, that *anyone* can make it ("check it out," they say, "we're here in medical school"). They believe that the attack of second-generation feminists on patriarchy, or even worse, *phallocentrism*, demonizes men and overstates their opposition to equality, and they are sick of what they see as feminism's male-bashing. None of this is terribly current: Kaminer (1995) posits that feminists have always been

> lampooned as sexually frustrated man haters (or impersonators) by defenders of the status quo. . . . Young women for whom sexual freedom is a more immediate concern than jobs are apt to focus on sexuality debates more than on demands for economic and political equity; to them, feminism must sometimes seem like an embittered, puritanical mother. (p. 22)

I think of a recent gathering of the Women in Medicine program here in my own setting when its members decided to turn away from issues of harassment and specialty discrimination in medicine (more of that "victim stuff" they want no part of) to "proactive" agendas that focus on leadership and what one highly respected, up-and-coming woman physician characterized as issues "any white male surgeon" would also relate to. I am stunned, especially in my own environment, at how myopic such thinking is, full of the hubris and the hardy individualism of those who have "arrived" and who mistakenly believe they have done so solely on their own merit. If they can do it, anyone can.

Clearly many young women in medicine (here, students) seated at the table of one of the most powerful, not to say conservative, cultural institutions in the Western world, believe that sexist oppression has for the most part been eradicated. Fifty percent is nothing to sneer at, nor is the incremental, albeit painfully slow movement of women into positions of power and prestige in the specialties and in academic hierarchies. But to ignore (in medicine, of all places!) that out there in the so-called real world the majority of women in the United States reside in pink-collar ghettos working in underpaid dead-end jobs; that women here and worldwide are yes, I'll say it, victims of exploitation and brutality ranging from domestic violence to rape to genital mutilation (the World Health Organization estimates the number of genitally mutilated women and girls at 80 million); that poor women (and men, and children) here and worldwide are denied the basic human right of adequate health care; and to think these are *not* the stuff of feminism—all this reeks with the nearsighted pride of those who have succeeded. Moreover, if those who criticize feminism/feminists so harshly had been doing their homework and had examined some of the women's studies scholarship they sneer at (Denfeld, 1995), they'd have found that feminists all over the world have quit thinking of gender as a unitary, static concept; that social class, race, age, and sexual orientation are all tangled up with gender as complex markers of human identity; that feminism has many, many styles and focused political passions.

In addition, many third-generation feminists have failed to identify and problematize the sites where feminist ideology and images of feminists themselves are produced, reproduced, and often distorted. Indeed, if one were to believe Denfeld, those of us in the academy have a lot more power than we ever dreamed possible in our women's studies classes and in our scholarly writing, where we (attempt to) mold the hearts and minds of young, impressionable women who come to these sites ostensibly without any prior beliefs about feminism. These students are portrayed as such poor thinkers that they confuse the content of the rich and varied "canon" of feminist theory with the requirement that they adopt said canon in toto if they are to call themselves feminists. (I think of Jocelyn Elder's fall from grace when the American public read her belief that masturbation should be examined as one dimension of sexuality as a call to "teach" children how to masturbate.) Feminism is about more than antipornography efforts or radical lesbian separatism, although it is deeply respectful and inclusive of each of these. Feminism, as Wendy Kaminer (1995) points out, has always been a collection of feminisms.

Many third-generation feminists, by ignoring the ever-widening call of feminists from all over the world to work collectively to end the various and ubiquitous oppression of women, have set up a straw woman in order to . . . what? and why? I am not sure I understand the implicit underpinnings of third-generation feminism, but I do have some hunches. It may have something to do with a generation raised by second-generation feminist mothers whose concerns now seem antiquated; with that same generation raised on the Reagan–Bush ideology, which can be characterized by denial practiced at new levels—denial of sexism, racism, and homophobia (remember Reagan's response to AIDS?); with the current conservative cultural ethos that views feminism's many agendas in opposition to that new cultural monolith, The Family; and with the return of the ferociously individualistic, we-don't-need-affirmative-action-anymore Horatio (Heloise?) Alger mythology currently circulating in the United States. Somehow, in the public mind, "when not being exploited to sell cigarettes, [feminism] got frozen in a stop-action photo of a furious, man-hating harpy ready to cut the balls off anything in sight" (Brookner, 1991, p. 11).

Whatever the explanations are, third-generation feminist perspectives seem to characterize the thinking of so many of the intelligent, highly focused, and altruistic women who are on the cusp of a demanding, prestigious career governed almost exclusively by men: They either do not identify themselves as feminists, or, if they do, they are very concerned about qualifying the label, most often with its possibility of being enacted with niceness and femininity. That's what *I* think, what I've observed and screened through my own beliefs and commitments.

But what do *they* say, these students of mine in a medical academy?

————

I interviewed twenty-four medical students, mostly in small groups of two to four. Fourteen were first- and second-year students; all but four were women. The students I interviewed were Euro-American, Asian or Pacific Islander, and African American. I interviewed the third- and fourth-year students singly or in pairs because of the difficulty I had in finding overlapping times in their schedules. Some of the students I knew from my classes; most I knew only by sight. I asked all of them the following questions, interspersed with clarifying questions or requests for elaboration:

How do you define feminism?
How did you arrive at that definition?
What do you see as the relationship between feminism and
    medicine?

Whatever preconceived notions I had for their answers were based on listening to women in my classes for the past 12 years, informal yet passionate conversations I had had with students outside class, and reading the theoretical (versus clinical) publications of women in academic medicine.

With the first question I sought students' definitions of *feminism*. Each group took on a rather distinctive character, based perhaps on the dialogue opened by the first student to speak. For example, Jill, the initial one to respond in a group of first-year students, provided a composite of her perception of a *feminist* rather than an elaboration on the ideology of feminism that the question posed; others followed her lead. "Anti" infused her definition, which she stated outright as the first word that came to her mind, followed by a disparate list: "abortion rights, ruckus, violent, extreme." Robin similarly listed characteristics of a feminist: "bra-burning, lesbian, college student, hates men, very liberal," yet posited that this was all changing, that feminism in the 1990s meant "using your femaleness to your power." One of the two men in the group, Sam, characterized feminism as "equity issues," beginning with the right to vote through the ERA, noting the current backlash and public perception that feminists have a "white male target." Wincing when Robin used the word *power,* he said her description sounded like "women doing guy pig-like things . . . that gives people an excuse to dismiss the movement." Robert saw two distinct sides of feminism: one political, the other artistic, preferring the latter because of its more subtle expression that can "get the point across" and have a "bigger impact."

Marcia, listening to this initial attempt to nail down a definition, began musing about "it," her inclusive term with hazy antecedent(s) ostensibly meaning sexism, which was her reading of the subject of feminism: "It's hard because I haven't entered the workplace yet . . . I haven't felt it . . . But I'm sure I'll feel it, like women in surgery. I hear, 'Don't go into surgery . . .'." She had heard from those ahead of her in the curriculum that the most troubling sources of sexism for medical students were clinical faculty. Indeed, her peers' advice included admonitions about aggressiveness ("white older men don't like aggressive women") and urgings to "be sweet and kiss butt." Robin disagreed, saying that she felt "it" now as a first-year student, but "it doesn't matter . . . my peers can't affect me . . . [they] have no power in my life." She was referring to the "objective" nature of evaluation in her classes, where tests are coded by numbers only, but she later reflected on troublesome gender dynamics with her peers in labs ("girls can't get a word in edgewise"). Here both Robin and Jill brought in cultural dimensions of male–female relations, believing that some of the "superior attitudes" of men in lab settings (with reciprocal passivity of many women to "play it out") should have ethnic or national origins factored into those gender relations. That is, they believed the origins of some of their male peers—many of them second generation in the United States—would explain some of the behaviors exhibited in classes and in social settings (for example, overheard by Robin in her dissection group, one male student to another: "I'd never marry a woman smarter than me"). Mindful of this intersection of ethnic identity and gender, Robin, Jill, and Marcia wondered about the various enactments of sexism in light of these other overlapping identities, but not without an aside that came close to blaming women themselves for such behaviors: Robin's observation that too many women have been taught that "you need a man to survive"; Marcia's observation of how many of her female peers buy into necessary female conditions of "prettiness and slimness"; and Jill's observation that she couldn't believe the number of "passive women [students]" she found in medical school. At this point Sam disagreed: "*All* medical students are taught to be passive, not just women."

With one exception, the ten third- and fourth-year women students I interviewed provided different observations on feminism from their younger peers. As a group, they thought more favorably of feminism and feminists. Julie, an articulate class leader at the start of her fourth year, characterized feminism as "standing up for all the differences (genetic, biological, learned) that are part of being a woman . . . [and] appreciating the role of women." Ann called it "empowering women . . . believing in the power of women [but] not about the use or abuse of power . . . women being recognized as human beings in the full sense of the word." Therese called it "a position you take championing the cause of women"; Madhavi called it an "inner strength that men just don't have." Two spoke candidly about essential female–male differences. Julie believed that women have an "innate nurturing, more holistic nature"; Madhavi believed that women have the ability "to do a whole bunch of roles at once—work, activities at home" and "to function in a woman's world *and* a man's world," a strength that "men don't have." She also used the words *instinctive* and *bonding* to characterize women's understandings of other women, yet she made it clear that to be a feminist didn't necessarily dictate overt political activism in women's organizations but was, rather, more a demeanor or an awareness that was "not necessarily outspoken." Indeed, she believed that it was a kind of "retro" version of feminism that was characterized by "*take, take, take . . . now* to be feminist is to *negotiate.*" Nina, the only student who spoke in negative terms about feminism, claimed the word connoted to her "meanness and crudeness." At this point and elsewhere in the interview, Julie repeated her one reproachful observation on feminists alongside her otherwise positive portrayal: how some feminists "exploit" their femaleness by "playing both sides . . . they use seductiveness, then complain. You can't be too sweet and then turn around and be tough, or talk out of both sides of your mouth."

What were the sources of their conceptions of feminism? Several cited their mothers more as role models than purveyors of feminist ideology. All students (with the one exception of Therese, a fourth-year student) recognized but did not problematize the inclusive term *media* as a major sledgehammer in feminist image construction, nor did they question who the media represent, whose interests they serve, who benefits from the perceptions evoked by their representations, and who loses. Ann was the most reflective here, disclosing her personal evolution as a feminist (including all-women secondary and higher education) and how she read the current cultural perceptions of feminism that seemed to be linked to the perceived excesses of the 1960s: "very skewed, very radical, real bizarre . . . bull dyke lesbian stuff," adding how most people "don't have a clue" that feminism is, among other things, about "single and married moms just trying to work in decent jobs."

The kind of feminism students believe has a place in medical education is the kind attuned to equity issues, also known as liberal feminism. Mona, a first-year student, claimed a feminist presence in medicine "should work for equity and nothing more" because generational and cultural differences in attending physicians make women's presence in medicine "complicated." Neeraj, another first-year student, called the "Asian population in medicine socially conservative . . . I even have some Indian friends whose moms don't drive." Mona agreed. "It's weird," she said, "with so many Indian women in medicine, a traditionally male profession, that the perceptions of 'women's place' is so conservative even among even my family and friends."

According to fourth-year Ann, such conservatism is pervasive in contemporary U.S. culture. Just as "white folks have not been taught to recognize racism, men (and many women) have not been taught to recognize sexism . . . it is still acceptable to be sexist." Yet a feminist presence in medicine "could do medicine a lot of good. . . . There are still too few women administrators, faculty, and deans, even with 40% of most classes being women. It's sorta like being a member of the country club just because your husband is. You've got the title and privileges, but not as much authority."

Therese believed that feminism will continue to "improve medicine . . . medicine will consider women's perspectives, do more about women's health, more research, and the research will get better as more and more women enter the field." Julie and Nina believed that feminism is one of the sources of a "team approach to medicine," that being "less antagonistic" [than men] is a "gift" women bring to medicine. Both unabashedly believed that women practice medicine differently from men.

––––––––––

What are some meanings we might derive from these medical students' words? I find several.

First, I am struck with many of the students' images of the personal qualities (including the bodies) of *feminists*, which they gave in response to my query regarding the definition of *feminism*. This is not an uncommon phenomenon. Consider the familiar expression that illustrates women's ideological agreement with feminist attitudes but unwillingness to self-label themselves feminist: "I'm not a feminist but . . . . " Wallis (quoted in Cowan et al., 1992) reported figures from a Yankelovich Clancy Shulman survey that indicated that 77% of the women surveyed believed the women's movement had bettered women's lives, 82% thought the movement was still improving women's lives, yet only 33% identified themselves as feminists.

Looking further into these differences, Cowan decided to use a communications model of persuasion to examine self-labeling and feminism. According to this model, willingness to identify oneself as a member of a social movement includes "*attitudes* toward the communicators, the *message* of the movement, and the *context* in which the message occurs" (Cowan et al., p. 323). Here, feminists are the communicators, the message is the values advanced by feminists, and the context is the actual social movement itself. Cowan proposes that "feminist self-labeling should be related to agreement with feminist thinking, [but] it may also be related to perceptions of the feminist movement and to . . . feminists themselves" (p. 323). That is, one can align oneself with the principles of gender equality but not necessarily want to affiliate with the movement itself because of negative perceptions of feminists. These images, almost all of them extremely negative, might be explained in part by relentless images, from the popular culture/media at large to the neighborhood pulpit. The historical underpinnings of this antifeminist campaign are far beyond my intentions for this work, yet I cannot help wondering not so much why students do not self-identify as feminists but rather why venomous portrayals of feminists have been so unproblematically accepted by students, women in particular, especially since it is feminists' labors that have permitted large numbers of women students to *be* here now.

Second, Cowan and her co-investigators proposed another explanation that may have bearing on why medical students generally do not self-identify themselves as feminists. This has to do with how one views the significance of individual versus group action, "whether individuals see their outcomes as individually or collectively determined. Feminism represents a collective social movement in which the causes of concern to women exist outside themselves and the solutions are social, not personal" (p. 323). That is, if one is to label oneself a feminist, the chances are quite good one would look to or at least be sympathetic to collective rather than individual action to solve problems. I make no earth-shattering revelation to anyone involved in medical education when I point out that medical students are most often highly competitive, individualistic people. Thus they may be less likely to form or join collective alliances aimed at erasing social injustices, especially if they don't see the need for its existence anymore (they already occupy a privileged space and often believe that hard work alone guarantees mobility and other rewards). Moreover, as my colleague Valerie Gilchrist, a doctor and a feminist, tells me, "Most people go into medicine to *do* medicine, not to fix the world." Thus the fixing, caring for, and helping that doctors do take place on microlevels between doctor and patient.

Third, the importance many medical students attach to niceness and negotiation also stands out in the interviews. With one exception, the several students who were willing to identify with the feminist movement believe that today's feminists have (or should have) these attributes. Never mind that contemporary feminist theorizing (outside medicine) continues to push language to new limits; to question and critique received cultural traditions, canons, epistemologies, or methodologies; and yes, to be confrontative: These students wanted a kinder and gentler feminism.

This move may be an explanation for why a number of students responded by saying *women* are more apt to do this or think that rather than using the word *feminist*. Women: a far more agreeable and acceptable tag within our culture and certainly within institutions than the feminist label. Yet I do not believe these students use the word interchangeably; rather, they consciously (or unconsciously) select the less emotionally and politically charged word. It may be that when they answered questions on feminism with "women doctors," often with energy and enthusiasm, they were expressing a clear interest in gender issues in medicine that was more politically acceptable and personally satisfying to them than talking about feminism and the baggage the feminist label often carries.

Moreover, they were remaining faithful to the patriarchal scripts of the U.S. medical academy, where intruders are admitted only if they join the "team" of those who govern the organization, write the rules, confer rewards and punishments. Individuals who do not subscribe to team politics—self-identified, openly ideological feminists—pose a threat to the morale of the team, the privileged space it occupies, and the rewards (status, money, etc.) team players receive. Learning and using the scripts becomes second nature, so that by the time they exit medical school, young doctors may actually have difficulty accessing those other scripts they once knew, especially those of anyone outside the adequately insured—the "undeserving" poor or the unmarried teen mother, for example.

What has happened with women in academia is a microcosm of what has happened with women in society—and it is what always happens, historically: a few are let in so that there are a few women in visible positions who can be pointed to as evidence that women have made it. . . . This means that much of what has succeeded in academia has been allowed to succeed because it's the kind of feminism institutions can live with.

—Gayle Greene, "Looking at History"

So, "what's feminism got to do with it?" With medical students? With teaching medical students? A great deal, in spite of students' qualified acceptance of, ambivalence toward, or dismissal of feminism.

Conceived narrowly, medical scripts pretend to be apolitical and neutral from the world outside the shelter of examining, operating, and emergency rooms, even if the patients found there are often inscribed with the inequities and injustices of that world. Conceived broadly, medicine is full of ambiguity, subjectivity, and risk as it traffics back and forth between the clinic and the world where the people it serves actually live. In fact, as Howard Waitzkin (1991) proposes, when physicians fail to confront or criticize the *social context* of the problems patients bring to the medical encounter (which include the myriad problems women face living in a sexist culture), they implicitly or explicitly generate the dominant ideology that may be the source of their patients' suffering.

Does this mean that all medical students, male and female, must self-identify as feminists to work against sexism? Of course not. Feminists who came of age in the second wave of feminism (the time of my own feminist awakening) may think about feminism differently, or wear the badge more proudly, or talk the talk more urgently and yes, loudly, than young feminists today, certainly more than the self-identified third-generation feminists. But if we really believe that feminism is an inclusive collection of ideologies, agendas, and theories working together toward a common goal, then third-generation feminists (and those working for social change in gender relations who may not even call themselves feminist) are to be included in that collective. This is one of the impressions I take away from listening to my students: Failing to label oneself a feminist is not necessarily positioning oneself against the various and multiple agendas of feminism. (I say wryly: "A rose by any other name . . .")

Still, I am concerned that in their fatigue with "victim" feminism, third-generation feminists position themselves as "victor" feminists,[2] the ones who have arrived and are comfortably nestled in places of respect, or authority, or financial rewards previously inaccessible to women. A bit like students who have won (deservedly, I say) a place in one of our culture's most prestigious professions, then exhibit the "bad faith of abandoning social justice work for others when [they are] already the beneficiary of partial social change" (Welch, 1990, p. 15).

Well *of course* we all cannot leave the academy and clinic and take to the streets as feminist activists. But we can recognize that there is work that remains unfinished in and outside medical settings having to do with the quality of life for women as both providers and patients, and we can honor those who do such work, *including feminists*. Without some sense of solidarity, too few of the "spoils traditionally monopolized by men would be available to any women at all. For women, and minority males, cooperation is not simply a utopian ideal, it's a practical necessity" (Kaminer, 1990, p. 7). Finally, we can acknowledge among ourselves and with our students that *we did not make ourselves* but have had, along with all the hard work that got each of us where we are today, the help of women before us and many who work beside us today.

5

Feminist Criticism in Literature and Medicine

We always "see" from points of view that are invested with our social, political and personal interests, inescapably "centric" in one way or another, even in the desire to do justice to heterogeneity.
> —Susan Bordo, "Feminism, Postmodernism, and Gender-Scepticism"

I really am looking for new narratives to replace the old ones. I distrust words and stories and yet probably they are what I value most. Paradox rules.
> —Lynne Tillman, "Critical Fiction/Critical Self"

AT A RECENT annual meeting of those who teach humanities in medical settings, I was seated in a large room listening to a well-known and highly regarded ethicist when, as an aside, he said we needed to do a "quick Rawls read." Most of the audience—white, middle-class, well-educated, big fish in the little pond of the medical humanities—politely laughed, participating in the coded familiarity of the so-called Great Conversation, which enabled us to connect John Rawls with the theory of justice that he developed. At that moment we were engaged in a rather harmless form of academic posturing, if we didn't consider those in the audience unfamiliar with Rawls (who, I assume, felt a bit illiterate). OK, I said to myself as I tried to diminish the effect of his words, it is just one offhand remark in the midst of a large meeting, not deeply symbolic of some larger, systemic design. But I heard very little of the remaining paper.

It's happening, I thought. The medical humanities, which emerged several decades ago as an outsider discourse in relation to medicine, seem to be almost assimilated into medicine, rather than hovering around its borders. The magnetic, persuasive power of medicine has transformed the medical humanities into one more academic department in the directory on the wall, with tight security at the borders of the knowledge in each discipline represented. This, of course, is probably viewed with satisfaction by some. But from where I'm situated, this assimilation has slowly distorted and now seeks to control the nature and purpose of our work. No longer on the outside, humanities inquiry in medicine has ceased to be unruly, confrontative, and daring. In the past such inquiry would unravel rather than connect, agitate rather than steady, disturb rather than reassure.

I have been thinking about this transformation a great deal lately, as I listen to my colleagues at meetings and read their essays in journals. I wonder how a "quick Rawls read" is translated back home in our classes of medical students and residents who are struggling to make meaning of their medicalized lives and how it symbolizes much of the scholarly activity in the medical humanities. But mostly, I am troubled as I reflect on my own teaching, trying to find meaning and purpose in this still strange land of literature and medicine. I believe that humanities inquiry—literature in particular—can confront, critique, and unsettle learners. With that as a goal, my literature classes should be sites of uneasiness, of exploding preconceptions, of self-conscious examinations of values and beliefs. My classes should be sites of resistance of the taken-for-granted, a place where our thinking and actions are under scrutiny. As such, these classes should not employ any method of literary study based solely on what Messer-Davidow (1989) describes as "differential, integral, principled, causal, inferential, and analogical thinking . . . [used] to classify, interpret, and judge literary works" (p. 87). Nor should our theorizing and discourse in the medical humanities reflect these methods of inquiry as the only legitimate means of exchanging and creating knowledge. Similarly, we should turn a critical gaze at the literature and medicine canon, or those whose worlds are informed only by Rawls (and the narrow Western philosophical tradition), or those who posture that their teaching and scholarship are not political events.

What are the alternatives? Literary study can be structuralist, poststructuralist, Marxist, historicist, deconstructionist, and various combinations of these and others. I offer one alternative among many: I propose that the medical humanities, literature in particular, be an outsider discourse in medicine that challenges inequities, distortions, and abuses of power. The textual analyst in this discourse is, then, a social analyst who identifies the "different lines of force in a text . . . [that] promote the interests of the socially dominant" (Fiske, 1995, p. 332). Such inquiry would explicitly and directly challenge the insidious, cunning, but often covert sexism, racism, classism, and heterosexism of our culture, all reflected in the practice of medicine in the United States. As one way to move literary inquiry to an outsider discourse, I propose that we turn to feminist criticism to help our resistance to oppressive structures. Such a turn may help us rethink the security of our present practice that seems to have been blessed, not merely by foundational knowledge governing the humanities disciplines that brought us to medicine in the first place, but by the customs, rituals, and hierarchies of academic medicine.

How might this work? Feminist criticism requires that we stand in a different relationship to the entities we study. Lillian Robinson (1978) presents one of the most helpful descriptions of the inclusiveness of feminist criticism—the way I use the term throughout this paper—by defining *feminist criticism* as criticism with a cause, criticism that seeks to end the oppressive effects of literature on people not only by the way it interprets or evaluates literary texts, but also by revolutionizing the institutions of literature, criticism, and education.

Moreover, when we acknowledge that as diverse knowers we are self-conscious and other-conscious, we can insert our perspectives and agencies into literary study. Knowing, then, becomes a collective quest grounded in experience, and experience is validated as we weave self-narratives into critical argument. Knowledge and knowledge making move away from definitive, freestanding constructs to cooperative, provisional formulations. Feminist inquiry, Messer-Davidow continues, views any knowledge as inadequate that censures or ignores the experiences and perspectives and persons of most of the human race.

A counterpatriarchic practice implicitly informs feminist criticism. Patriarchy is, of course, linked to the systematic control of men over women, but it is also related to other forms of oppression. Thus a counterpatriarchic practice has a strong relevance to other struggles against unjust relations based on race, class, sexual orientation, national origins, and so on. This cannot be overstated here: A counterpatriarchic practice, implicit in the various feminisms, resists the subjugation of women but is also committed to countering oppression of all people. If understanding the multiplicity and diversity of lived experience is a goal of a just and caring medical practice, then examining and challenging any oppressive custom that undermines such caregiving should be a primary goal of literary inquiry in medical settings.

How might all this fit into our current practice of teaching literature and medicine and our way of talking about our classroom practice? This is difficult to answer; our teaching is diverse because we who teach literature and medicine are a diverse group. But it is safe to say that feminist criticism in literature and medicine is not silent about any patriarchal practice of medicine. Susan Sherwin has similarly written about medical ethics, that "the deep questions about the structure of medical practice and its role in a patriarchal society are largely inaccessible within the [medical ethics] framework" (1992b, p. 23). In contrast, feminist criticism howls: It does not tiptoe or whisper; it does not automatically canonize the ways of knowing approved by medicine. Rather, it is interested in working quite literally from the outside, going no further "in" than the borders between literature and medicine, resisting the pull to enter the inner circle of medicine as the only site of legitimacy or sanction. Feminist criticism does not appropriate competing narratives indiscriminately, a practice that is, according to Rosemary Hennessy (1993), the dominant mode of reading in the academy today. Such eclecticism, which "uncritically links explanatory frames without making visible the contesting assumptions on which they are often premised . . . [obstructs] the ways the production of the social real in language shapes and is in turn shaped by divisions of labor and formations of state . . . as well as . . . the ways meaning is the effect of social struggle" (p. 15). Finally, feminist criticism is a "mode of praxis. . . . [Its] point is to change the world" (Schweickart, 1986, p. 38); such practice in medicine would be, unabashedly, to change all morally unacceptable medical practice.

Thus I posit that feminist criticism become one alternative framework for teaching literature in medical settings, whereby issues illuminated by literature take readers deeper into the personal and political domains, where teachers and students together engage in heretical questioning of patriarchal practices, norms, standards, or rules, spoken or implicit, in both the culture at large and in the medical culture reflecting and inscribing those thoughts/practices. Such a framework is not based on medicine- or canon-bashing, or on dismissing all Western philosophical traditions. I often and gleefully use works found predictably in many literature and medicine syllabi, and insist on close, analytical readings of the texts I assign. I find traditional works important not because they represent eternal truths but because students can benefit from reading the works of such visionaries,

> to show them how to think, to teach them how to keep their minds open. And that is also the reason we need to include new voices in the curriculum—to show all students that they can participate, as thinkers, readers, writers, and critics, in the cultivation of new classics. The best way to honor our traditions is to extend them. (Beverly & Fox, 1989, p. 52)

Moreover, when we talk and write about our teaching, when we puzzle about these issues to each other, we can be freer to build from our personal experience in those classrooms, in what Nancy K. Miller calls the "witnessing 'I' of subjective experience . . . that shapes a variety of personal and less personal discourses at an oppositional angle to dominant critical positionings" (1991, p. 14).

As I reflect on many of the ideas suggested here, I have come to believe that teaching and research informed by feminist criticism may move us and our students to think about the taken-for-granted in classes, corridors, and conferences rooms; in relationships with patients; and in the institutions where we do our work. But in the following paragraphs I will narrow the discussion to how feminist criticism may confront and perhaps influence our thought and practice as we teach and talk about literature and medicine. I begin by telling a story about a literature and medicine class I teach, then step back to reflect on and critique the teaching and curriculum issues raised by this classroom episode. My discussion is necessarily and explicitly grounded in my feminist perspectives and commitments.

I was to begin a new class in a few days. In addition to rereading the literature I had assigned, I spent a great deal of time thinking about what I was going to say during that introductory class. The goal of the class, "Women's Health Issues in Literature," was to examine how selected literature works to portray major health events in most women's lives; how race, class, and sexual orientation may influence the experience of illness and the delivery of care; and how these literary depictions might deepen and enlarge students' perceptions of these issues and possibly compel them to work at oppositional and transformative angles to unjust social relations in medicine.

However, there was much, much more going on here for me than merely preparing for class. I wanted to make explicit from the beginning what the roaming, murmuring background was in all my classes, a background that was clearly feminist. I wanted this class to be a place to confront racism, sexism, classism, heterosexism, and other oppressive beliefs and acts in ourselves, in students' relationships with patients, in medical education (including this class), in hospitals and clinics. When I named myself feminist at the onset, I hoped to explain how that position might influence what went on in class. I wanted to do so not as some act of bravado, or to focus attention on myself in a kind of solipsistic teacher confessional or testimonial. Rather, I wanted to establish an atmosphere with my students that would focus our thinking and our relationships with one another and with patients in a way that might call into question prescribed, medicalized postures of authoritative and categorical thought. Of course, I thought I had worked toward this during my twelve years of teaching literature and medicine. Yet, as I uneasily reflected back on this teaching, I was not so sure.

With all this in mind, I began the new class. I told students how the class had been simmering for several years as I became more aware of the disparities between clinical accounts of women's health issues and women's lived accounts of these experiences, often startlingly portrayed in fiction. I disclosed how my feminism fueled what I saw, heard, and read in my medical surroundings. I detailed how literature could be studied as it focused attention on the following: cultural inequities; where we stood in relation to oppressive beliefs and acts; what we were willing to do regarding oppressiveness we enacted and witnessed; what all this might mean in the larger medical system that perpetrated differential treatment based on race, gender, sexual orientation, and ability to pay. I also revealed my worries: how I might unknowingly silence or shame students who did not share my explicit zealotry; how I could be enacting in less overt form what any number of intolerant clinicians or professors demanded daily on teaching rounds in hospitals. I revealed that we would be talking often about what was going on in class, and I earnestly invited them to speculate about how my professorial privilege would interfere with honest self-disclosure on their part regarding a subject so obviously critical to me. Many students nodded, all were silent, most looked uneasy or a bit embarrassed at this monologue. I was uneasy, too, so we moved on into discussion of the literature I had assigned for this class.

The topics were birth, abortion, miscarriage, and infertility. We read and discussed poetry by Linda Pastan, Lucille Clifton, and Sharon Olds, and a short story by Margaret Atwood. We searched for meanings in the language of fiction to tell the stories differently from clinical accounts and conventional knowledge of medicine: What did this woman think when she looked down in the toilet and saw the remnants of her pregnancy—"clots of blood . . . Dark red like black in the salty / translucent brine"? (Olds, 1984, p. 25). Or what about this mother's cynical description of a contemporary U.S. delivery room, where she was "strapped down / victim in an old comic book"? (Pastan, 1982, p. 26). A spirited discussion surrounded these poems, and I, the only nonmedical person in the room, became voyeur once again through my students' accounts of what they see daily in hospitals.

Then the difficulties began. We read aloud an excerpt from Toni Morrison's (1970) novel, *The Bluest Eye*, which focuses on the early life of Pauline, a relentlessly poor, sad woman trapped in a lonely life and an unhappy marriage who decides to go to the hospital to have her second child, Pecola, rather than have her at home as she did with her firstborn. While the story takes place over 50 years ago, we still cringed at the cruel overtness of the racist male doctor who, at Pauline's bedside, remarks casually to the young doctors rounding with him, "These here women you don't have any trouble with. They deliver right away and with no pain. Just like horses" (p. 99)—a common script of the era reflecting not only medicine but the culture in which it was practiced. Only one of the younger doctors looked at Pauline's face, and when he did, she knew that he was ashamed at what he had just witnessed. He knew, Pauline thought, that she was no mare foaling, but he didn't respond and silently moved on with the rest of them as they began examining a white woman nearby, fussing over her, asking her how she was doing. Pauline's pains get worse, and she starts moaning "something awful" even though the pains aren't as bad as she is letting on. But she needs to let everyone know that

> I hurt just like them white women. Just 'cause I wasn't hooping and hollering before didn't mean I wasn't feeling pain. What'd they think? That just 'cause I knowed how to have a baby with no fuss that my behind wasn't pulling and aching like theirs? (p. 99)

One young woman, a fourth-year student, started to describe her experiences during her obstetrics/gynecology rotation. Much of her training during this rotation (currently true for many medical students in the United States) had been in ob/gyn clinics in hospitals. Her remarks turned the discussion away from Pauline to herself, even as she continued to speak on the subject of oppression. As the discussion unfolded and other students joined in, I learned the pejorative way "clinic patient" or "house patient" was often used: poor women/girls. Mostly black. Frequent drug/alcohol involvement. Multiple births. Noncompliant. Many with an "attitude." Few remarks commingled these *characterizations* of clinic patients with the *oppression* of clinic patients in terms of access, silencing, and other acts of medical marginalization.

Then more descriptions, more scripted representations without students' concomitant acknowledgment of their part in the domination of these patients: "I lost count of how many pregnant 15-year-olds I saw who already had children"; "Clinic patients are less compliant"; "Clinic patients wait too long to get medical care." Then students' self-disclosures: "I was jaded within a week"; "It's hard to feel compassion for them"; or "I have to make myself go in there and try to give them the same care I would give to the CEO's wife, but it's tough."

I was speechless. I heard students revealing some very intimate feelings that deeply affected their roles and responsibilities as physicians. This was, after all, part of what I had hoped for all along: for us to identify oppressions, to see ourselves as victims *and* perpetrators of oppressions, and to come to a point where we were able to confront and oppose those oppressions. But many of these young doctors, now in the trenches taking care of people whose lives are broken and covered with the fallout of a culture that denigrates and ignores their very existence, viewed these clinic patients clearly as Other. They felt empathy for Pauline when they were reading and discussing the story, but they did not make a link between Pauline and their own patients, or between Pauline's doctor(s) and their own doctoring.

Still, I said very little during the discussion, and as the class ended, I was baffled, frustrated, and silent as students left the room. It took me days of thinking and talking with several colleagues to identify the obvious. I realized that in the clinical scenarios they provided in response to *The Bluest Eye*, students identified *themselves* as the victims, put in situations where they felt unprepared and overwhelmed, confronted with humans whose lives were alien to what most of them had ever experienced. In their frustration, exasperation, and inability to understand, *they* were the exploited ones in a medical system that sloughed off care of the poor to the least experienced caregivers, who were themselves at the bottom of the heap in the caregiving hierarchy.

For it is there at the bottom that the legendary training ritual of *pimping* can be found, what most medical students and residents experience at one time or another: the cruel intellectual hazing carried out usually by the senior medical person—often the attending or senior resident—who relentlessly probes the novice for small and sometimes obscure details about this or that medical condition. Not quite a kick-the-dog phenomenon, but in the same family of response.

If such cruelty—regardless of tradition or intention—is carried out between and among doctors and students, how far behind could patients be? And given that medical students do not arrive at medical school without the same biases that plague us all; given that such biases are the nasty little secrets of all humans in all professions, including the caring ones; given that medical students are rarely given the chance to confront and reflect openly on their own and their profession's prejudicial beliefs and practices but are expected to cast them out early with the magical Hippocratic wand, it is no wonder that students responded in this way to the literature we read.

OPENLY IDEOLOGICAL TEACHING

The various feminisms, regardless of their particular orientations, are deeply committed to exposing and articulating the gendered nature of history, culture, and society. As a teacher who admits vulnerability and uncertainty in my teaching and writing, I struggle daily with what it means to bring my convictions openly into my classes and my relationships with students and colleagues. This is difficult to do, to name one's deeply felt commitments while guarding against pontification and encouraging a kind of group-think based on correct answers—an educative scenario that replaces one pattern of domination with another.

As Lather (1991) points out, Sandra Harding is helpful here when she distinguishes between the "coercive values" of racism, classism, and sexism, which distort and mystify our culture's explanations and understandings of difference, and the "participatory values" of antiracism, anticlassism, and antisexism, which honor, with authenticity and without patronizing, the individual human life. Those of us who teach literature and medicine, making explicit our commitment to participatory values, must be vigilant about the necessity of self-reflexivity, of examining how our presence permeates our classes in ways we might not intend, of discovering how we are in collusion with that which we critique in medicine. Lather (1991), describing her own openly ideological teaching and research, writes that "such a movement of reflexivity and historicity at once inscribes and subverts. Provisionality and undecidability, partisanship and overt politics, replace poses of objectivity and disinterestedness" (p. 10). Thus being open about our convictions—here, grounded in feminism(s)—mandates examination of how and what we teach with the intent of correcting "both the invisibility and distortion" of women's (and Others') experience, and to end their unequal social position (Lather, 1986, p. 68). Such teaching, then, makes it impossible to recede behind content or method, and such teaching is difficult, at least as I reflect on my own experiences in literature and medicine.

As the preceding classroom scenario indicates, I am engaged in a continuing, reflective, often difficult critique of my teaching. Focusing back on the women students in class, I try to understand how they have been rewarded for passivity and indoctrinated in stereotypical sex roles in all of their educational experiences. I try to identify my complicity as a teacher in promoting a sexist, racist, classist, heterosexist education. I look at the daily examples of our lives as teachers, doctors, administrators in patriarchic settings (medical schools, hospitals, medical practices), and how this informs students and residents about our values and beliefs. I scrutinize our actions with our women students in formal and informal teaching situations—not merely our overt and subtle exchanges, but how we listen to our women students. Again I read Adrienne Rich's "Taking Women Students Seriously" and find it as sadly relevant today as it was a dozen years ago when it was written. I quote at length because of her startlingly accurate portrayal of many women's educative experiences from early childhood through graduate education:

> Look at a classroom: look at the many kinds of women's faces, postures, expressions. Listen to the women's voices. Listen to the silences, the unasked questions, the blanks. Listen to the small, soft voices, often courageously trying to speak up, voices of women taught early that tones of confidence, challenge, anger, or assertiveness, are strident and unfeminine. Listen to the voices of the women and the voices of the men; observe the space men allow themselves, physically and verbally, the male assumption that people will listen, even when the majority of the group is female. Look at the faces of the silent, and of those who speak. . . . As women teachers, we can either deny the importance of this context in which women students think, write, read, study, project their own futures; or try to work with it. We can either teach passively, accepting these conditions, or actively, helping our students identify and resist them. (Rich, 1985, p. 27)

Yes, I have been looking for ways to help myself and my students resist, all of us victims and perpetrators of oppression. But we looked too little at our own complicity in cultural/medical power plays. In the class I described, the women students did identify oppression, but only others' enactment of it in the huge medical/cultural system of dominance, and stopped short of identifying their fit in the rest of the chain of domination where they unwittingly oppressed other women. On some levels, Rich's description was more relevant to the physician–patient relationship (perhaps we could rewrite it as "Taking Marginalized *Patients* Seriously") than it was to our classroom, where middle-class, highly educated women students recognized their own passivity and perceived powerlessness in the medical hierarchy. But the difference in the degree and kind of oppression between the women students and their women patients is obvious, in addition to the fact that women students know they will not be in their present place forever. Theirs was a resistance of silence and compliance to survive, to get out of the system to enter it again, the next time with the power they now lacked.

Lewis and Simon remind us that "oppression is enacted not by theoretical concepts but by real people in concrete situations" (1986, p. 469): on teaching rounds, in literature and medicine classes, in lectures and informal exchanges, and elsewhere. Students described their own oppressive behavior, which was not as overt as Pauline's physician's racism, yet they were unable or unwilling to examine how the subtle differences in care they give to clinic patients—unintentional and unconscious, I believe—were one more predictable, relentless enactment of power and privilege leveled against the disenfranchised.

But how to move beyond a sense of being powerless victims of medicine themselves? Although matter-of-fact about the inequities and injustices in their own medical education and in the clinical scenarios they witness and take part in every day, these medical students were still troubled and confused. Contrary to some current popular cynicism about doctors, medical students enter medicine full of energetic, altruistic idealism. As the realities of power and authority become routinized in their education, their will to survive the moment often transcends their social conscience; they are more like the young doctor who looks at Pauline's face, silently knowing yet moving on. Often it takes reading Pauline's story to remind students of what is behind the gazes of many of their patients.

Yes, it is true that in this particular class, Pauline did little more than trigger students' disclosures of life in the clinic. What *they* chose to identify as oppression—their own—was compelling and immediate. Their examination was quite above ground in a matter-of-fact blaming mode, never venturing below to their own enactment of power and oppression (where Professor wanted them to go). Still, I believe that literature, with its rich, unsettling ambiguities, can be a place to launch a critique of dominant positionings if we are able to examine—partial and biased as that examination will be—what lies below the murky surface of our teaching and doctoring. But in the midst of that discussion, I did not know how to venture there with students; I was too caught up in my position that kept me in my clean, antiseptic classroom, where I was clearly not the one touching and probing the bodies and minds of persons so different from me in clinics all across the city, as students are required to do. Moreover, my commitments not to engage in "you should/you shouldn't" with students, not to posture as the one with answers, washed away a critical moment in our class when a reflective, self-conscious critique of our beliefs and practice should have occurred.

Yet it is within these concrete situations that we as teachers can alter our postures, resulting in a discourse that appears objective and distanced; a single discourse that proclaims to be the locus of certainty, certification, legitimation; a discourse that is ultimately a vehicle for domination as we (clasping our disciplines/"expertise") pose as those who know what "they"—students and the marginalized they care for—need and want. Physician David Hilfiker talks of physicians confronting their own brokenness as they care for their very broken patients:

> We need to bring ourselves more into the process of healing, not just our expertise. . . . Doctors need to know how to really be able to feel their pa-

tients' pain. And the only way to be able to feel a patient's pain is by being willing to face your own. (1989, pp. 96–97)

Perhaps that is where Pauline and others like her can help us uncover not only the pain of patients, but our own pain. This is where I must learn to go with students, a place that is near *but is not the same* as their feelings of victimization by the medical system. Identifying their victimization is essential, and to gather enough courage to confront the medicalized system of domination would be an extraordinary measure, especially if it is enacted in multiple voices. But to leave out of that confrontation the difficult and puzzling recognition of the ways we/they dominate and oppress patients is to deny one of the many potentials for literary inquiry in medicine. My challenge was how to tie the unaffected, evocative immediacy of Pauline's experience (which students empathically identified with) to the clinic patients.

OPENLY IDEOLOGICAL CONTENT

Up to this point, I have tried to establish that grounding our teaching and theorizing about our practice with feminist underpinnings might encourage literary inquiry that explicates the following: readers' vulnerability and self-doubt; the subjectivity of their lived experience; their connections to the humans found in the texts they read; and, possibly later, a more authentic honoring and attempt to understand their patients' lives. It may be possible, then, for our literature classrooms to be catalysts for changes in the way we think about medicine, power, and oppression and to identify where we are each situated in this puzzling, tangled matrix.

Such activity, however, doesn't exist in a void of content, nor should it, in literature and medicine classes. *What* do we teach? What we select to read/discuss in our classrooms has the enormously understated power to generate different understandings; every piece we select for students to read reflects a political agenda. Here enters ambivalence, at least for many of us who teach literature. Many of us are products of, purveyors of, and still lovers of literature that, with precious few exceptions, excludes women, nonwhites, and non-Westerners. I have taught Mann, Tolstoy, Dostoyevsky, Camus, Chekhov, Kafka at every chance, and required William Carlos Williams and Walker Percy in all my classes—that is, some literary counterparts to Rawls in a philosophy class. My thinking and tastes were deeply set in these texts as the best source of culture, literacy, and the timeless struggles confronting all humans, so much that I was often hesitant to include in my syllabus literary possibilities found elsewhere for fear of excluding something "important." Through my literary exclusions, I "suppressed a conversation about the social order" (Craige, 1992, p. 14). And in doing so, I selected content that portrayed a kind of human essentialism that unproblematically seemed to universalize humans' lived experiences.

"We know ourselves," writes Leslie Marmon Silko, "by the stories we tell about ourselves" (quoted in Long, 1992, p. 3). Likewise, we get to know others by the stories we hear and read. The writer Bharati Mukherjee maintains:

> The most moving form of praise I receive from readers can be summed up in three words: *I never knew.* Meaning, I see these people (call them Indian, Filipino, Korean, Chinese) around me all the time and I never knew they had an inner life. (quoted in Long, 1992, p. 4)

When we thoughtfully select literature outside the literature and medicine canon, we bring into our awareness the dailiness, joy, and pain of people who have been made invisible by the dominant culture. Certainly the lives of Tolstoy's Ivan Ilych, or Kafka's Gregor Samsa, or Camus' Rieux provide extraordinary, provocative accounts of persons struggling to make sense and create meaning in their lives, accounts that may mirror or enlarge similar experiences of many readers. But what can these accounts tell us about a Native American woman raising her transracial child (Michael Dorris's [1987] *A Yellow Raft in Blue Water*), or a woman— a lesbian—confronting her breast cancer with her lover (Sandra Butler and Barbara Rosenblum's [1991] *Cancer in Two Voices*), or the enduring violence of incest to the body and spirit (Jane Smiley's [1991] *A Thousand Acres*)? These texts pull back the curtains for us to see and hear the living going on in lives we never considered.

Why is this important? Many doctors may never encounter a woman from Zaire, or a homeless family living in a car, or a gay man from Rio in their waiting rooms, or the kind of overt racism found in the obstetrics ward in Morrison's *The Bluest Eye*. Yet multiple voices are essential to developing the perspectivity and sensitivity needed to examine ourselves and others, and to engage in a critique of the oppressive thought and practice mirrored in our own lives, our institutions, and most assuredly in medical practice. Multiple perspectives are necessary to open up the borders on what can be imagined; they encourage ambiguity and multiplicity rather than order, structure, and univocality; they unlock what has been muted, repressed, and unheard. Multiple perspectives are vital to anyone in a profession providing care to other humans.

Of course the content we choose is inherently political. The required readings and the notions of what students "should" read masquerade as what is natural, rational, and necessary but are in the end politicized human productions that grant legitimacy to some voices while denying it to others. These readings embrace what Raymond Williams called the *selective tradition:* "someone's selection, someone's vision of legitimate knowledge and culture, one that in the process of enfranchising one group's cultural capital disenfranchises another's" (quoted in Apple, 1992, p. 5). Without the stories of Others whose experiences are outside our own, we have far less chance of recognizing their inner lives and lived experiences—essential awarenesses to caring for the persons inside broken or sick bodies.

Still, a critique of the content I currently select for my literature and medicine classes reveals other problems: I may contribute to the very conditions I work against. The women authors I include in my syllabus address only women's health/medical concerns: hysterectomy, breast cancer, miscarriage, infertility, birth, and abortion. The African-Americans I include in this group are Lucille Clifton, Alice Walker, Toi Derricotte, Gloria Naylor, and Toni Morrison; their stories and poems address *only* birth and abortion. Other significant life issues—aging; friendship and love; the meanings of health, dying, and suffering—are found in the words of mostly white, male, Western writers. When I try to be spokesperson for the Other, I sustain their Otherness by positioning them in stereotypical places, often victims without agency. bell hooks (1990) describes this phenomenon of attempting to speak for others as a way of thinking in a place of privilege that I pass on to students using literature as a means:

> No need to hear your voice when I can talk about you better than you can speak about yourself. No need to hear your voice. Only tell me about your pain. I want to know your story. And then I will tell it back to you in a new way. Tell it back to you in such a way that it has become mine, my own. Rewriting you, I write myself anew. I am still author, authority. I am still the colonizer, the speaking subject, and you are now at the center of my talk. (p. 152)

I inscribe the Otherness of women, poor women, women of color, and I thought I had been doing otherwise. As Diana Fuss characterizes it, I tried to "undo by overdoing" (1989, p. 86).

———

In the preceding pages, I have maintained that those of us who teach literature and medicine are not mandated to "expose" our students/residents to the selected tradition in literature and medicine. Instead, my proposition has been that we select and read literature that (1) portrays lives and experiences outside the dominant frames of knowing; (2) causes us to reflect on our own active or passive role in reproducing racist, sexist, heterosexist, classist, and other oppressive practices; (3) prompts us to change, to work in the service of the feminist commitment to end the exploitation and oppression of all humans. Because feminist criticism is tied to transforming literary inquiry and the larger culture itself, I have argued for feminist underpinnings to anchor our teaching and our talk.

Everything on which these beliefs rests is based on a premise that has, I hope, been an implicit thread weaving its way throughout this chapter: that literature has the power to make things happen, that it can help us to "think beyond our limits, while acknowledging limits" (Tillman, 1991, p. 102). Reading literature in medical settings may inspire us to examine our unspoken beliefs, to do what we never thought about doing, to do what we must to provide care that *is* caring and inclusive. It has to do with Maxine Greene's image of what education might be on any level, in any domain,

> conceived as a process of futuring, of releasing persons to become different, of provoking persons to repair lacks and to take action to create themselves. . . . This means that one's "reality," rather than being fixed and predefined, is a perpetual emergent, becoming increasingly multiplex, as more perspectives are taken, more texts are opened. . . . [It is] a vision of education that brings together the need for wide-awakeness with the hunger for community. (1988, pp. 22–23)

This image is possible even in medical settings if we, too, think about what we're doing when we teach literature and medicine—why we teach, how we teach, what we teach.

As I look back to where I started, I offer the following scenario. I am seated in a large room at a conference with my colleagues who teach humanities in medical settings. A well-known and highly respected ethicist, a woman, has just given an aside, suggesting that we do a quick Sandra Harding read, or any of the countless feminist philosophers of science writing outside canonical boundaries. The audience laughs politely, because they, like the speaker, are well grounded in outsider discourses; they know Rawls, yes, but they also think of philosophy (and literature, and science, and other provinces of knowing) as disciplines that are informed by perspectives far more inclusive than those predictable ones we've all been provided in the academy where men still claim discursive authority, past and present. And while she's up there talking, she's telling us about her teaching and theorizing in a consciously first-person autobiographical stance. She is engaged in what Mary Ann Caws calls a "willing, knowledgeable, outspoken involvement . . . with the subject matter" and extends to her listeners (and her students) an invitation to "participate in the interweaving and construction of the ongoing conversation" (quoted in Miller, 1991, p. 24). She leads us, as bell hooks (1992) describes it, "back to where it all began, to that moment when a woman or child, who may have thought she was all alone, began feminist uprising, began to name her practice, began to formulate theory from experience" (p. 82).

Yes, there is still posturing going on here, but each time we redraw or enlarge the boundaries of our knowing, richer, more abundant, more imaginative thinking is likely to occur. I sketch this scenario not to replace little boy philosophers chuckling with one another about Rawls with little girl feminist critics chuckling with one another about Harding. I envision this because I do not live and teach in a vacuum. I have deep regard for my colleagues and my peers; their thinking startles, questions, and informs me as I continue my own life's work of teaching and working at socially transformative angles in a medical academy. I think, learn, study, read, and teach, not just in my 20th-century educated Western web, but in the smaller intellectual community of these scholars and teachers of the medical humanities and, most importantly, in that location where all our knowledge, skills, and values come together with those we are ultimately there to serve: in the classroom with our students. Our theoretical discourse is important to me, but I want the discourse to be more inclusive, just as I want my teaching to be more inclusive of persons/patients underrepresented, forgotten, or ignored by the culture that informs current medical practice. Maxine Greene (1987) concludes:

> [T]his may be, in the last analysis, what seems to connect artistry and teaching—this effort to open out of the commonplace, out of the cotton wool of habit and dailyness, to discover (in our plurality, in our human being together) what it is like to look at things as if they could be otherwise and somehow learn enough to actualize that otherwise in decency—and then to move beyond. (p. 14)

6

Teaching Difference in the Medical Academy

There go your precious "theys" again. They wouldn't understand—not in Detroit, not on Brewster Place, not anywhere! And as long as they own the whole damn world, it's them and us, Sister—them and us. And that spells different!

—Gloria Naylor, *The Women of Brewster Place*

IN BOTH my teaching and research in the medical academy, I have spent many years questioning what *difference* means: differences in race, gender, social class, sexual desire; epistemic differences, especially those between art and science and their respective methodologies; differences between truth and knowledge, power and knowledge. My search is to locate ways to break down unjust social relations that exploit power differentials implicit in dualistic thinking: Science is valued more than art, reason more than emotion, masculine more than feminine, the haves more than the have-nots, white more than other colors.

Some of the many dualisms that I work against are those having to do with race, with white and not white, and how color is woven into the complexities of gender and class structure in the United States. I struggle with what it means to be a white, middle-class feminist working against oppressive social structures. This labor includes finding ways to understand more fully the meanings of my whiteness; that is, how I interpret it, how it has been constructed historically, how others who are not white may perceive it, and how these understandings are implicitly forwarded to others in my teaching and research. Moreover, I work to uncover the particular understandings I bring to the intersection of race, gender, and class. My knowledge of gender is based on my own material and embodied experience of being a woman in a capitalist society that places value on whiteness and maleness. The other dimensions of oppression in that same culture I have learned in a more disembodied way: in history, story, and myth; in the ubiquitous signs and manifestations of popular and academic culture; in the daily empiricism of being awake and aware.

As a teacher and scholar I participate in the academic discourse of race and ethnicity in ways that are both known and unknown to me. Until mid-century, this discourse was unapologetically candid in its support of the "intellectual, cultural, political and moral superiority" of white, Western civilization over everyone else, everywhere (van Dijk, 1993, p. 159). Today the discourse is wrapped in the kinder and gentler terms of cultural diversity, the ostensibly unbiased approach that provides an extensive laundry list of traits or characteristics of nondominant groups, from time orientation to family structures to patterns of eye contact. The hidden message here is that anything that does not blend easily with the dominant way of doing things is secondary to it and needs to be learned with a codified, categorical neatness so caregivers do not do anything to offend those who do not know or subscribe to these dominant cultural habits.

In the mass media, much is written about the economic and employment status of nonwhites, invasions of refugees depleting this country's economic resources, violent inner cities, drug-infested housing projects, welfare abusers. Certainly such accounts contribute directly to racist resentment among whites.[1] But what about the more subtle, rarely examined racism embedded in privileged discourses of the scientific community, the modern corporation, the military, and, yes, the medical academy? I am not referring to the sensational theories of sociobiology or psychobiology appearing with some regularity that suggest hereditary properties of race and intelligence. What I am looking for—in myself and elsewhere in the medical academy—are instances of "collusion, passivity, inaction, or failure to combat prejudice and discrimination" (van Dijk, p. 26). That is, I am trying to understand not if, but how, we reproduce racism in the medical academy.

This inquiry leads me to particular circumstances in which race and class are examined in the medical school curriculum where I have been working for over a dozen years; my observations are, of course, biased and partial. As I try to understand the reproduction of racism in my environment, I have selected the concept of *essentialism*[2] to guide my inquiry. Essentialism emerges in the medical academy in many locations, much of it subtly expressed in the ethos of the institution, some of it under the various curricular attempts at diversity or multiculturalism. Discussions of race and class, both critical factors influencing the doctor–patient relationship, are often imbued with essentialist claims that suggest categorical, unitary attributes of, say, blacks, the poor, or the indigent. Somewhere deep in the psyche of a racist, fiercely individualist culture, such groups are assumed to be connected by biology or nature, or other given characteristics such as intelligence, social practice, or emotional response, making them easy to sort or classify. Moreover, essentialist thinking about groups imposes limits on variations within those groups, thus reinforcing expectations that make it unlikely that a member of a group will behave in a way contrary to his or her group's characteristics.

In a culture that values white skin, essentialist beliefs about persons with nonwhite skin are deeply enmeshed in our thinking, often acting as explanations or excuses for the continued social and economic oppression of those who are not white.[3] However, some of these same groups, usually those who are marginalized in some way, also use essentialist thinking to their advantage. These groups have found that working together from a common point of origin—race, gender, sexual desire, for example—is a powerful strategy for social change. The attendant risks remain, however, when any group exercising identity politics is perceived from within and without to be a monolithic "natural" entity. But as bell hooks reminds us, there is an enormous difference between *choosing* the margins as a space for radical critique and being put there, which is one of the reasons many groups "take the risk" of essentialism for political strength in numbers.

Thus, throughout my discussion I question whiteness—the racialized bedrock on which the medical academy was built in the United States and on which it remains historically situated at all levels[4]—and some of its manifestations and meanings in medical education, especially assumptions of whiteness in the teaching of difference. I focus on two areas where medical students often find explicit attention given to race and class, fertile ground for essentialism: (1) in the various places we teach students about doctor–patient relationships, especially as they learn to take a history, and (2) in the medical humanities, a literature class in particular. In both I look for hidden or unintentional essentialist dimensions of these curricular efforts, examining not necessarily the "goodness" or "badness" of essentialism but rather how and why it is evoked, trying all the while to understand how it is manifested in an institution dedicated to the education of caring, socially conscious physicians.

(SOME) ESSENTIALIST BIASES SHAPING MEDICAL EDUCATION

Early Signs

Various forms of essentialist thought can be found throughout the medical academy, often in unlikely places. Moves toward this form of categorical thinking can be found early in the curriculum when students meet their cadaver, a body without a name, now without the lived experience of being a daughter, mother, lover, or friend. Rather, it is a body on which anatomy is learned, a body that readily becomes Everyman. Later in lectures and texts the cadaver is replaced by the "70-kilogram man," who comes to represent Everypatient, generalizable regardless of gender or race or socioeconomic status.

Such a push to think in terms of a universal human body easily leads to abstractions, categories, and principles regarding our collective humanness, a humanness that includes far more than anatomy and physiology. Such a push, it can be argued, can lead to essentialism, which involves not just imaging a prototypical patient but also codifying how that patient should look, act, and think about medicine, health, and illness. Norms must be established for Everypatient, but these are not just norms of height and weight, blood counts or respiration rates, but of roles to be played out in the doctor–patient relationship. Here is power at work: Doctor is possessor and dispenser of knowledge, an entity who is to be listened to and whose directions are to be followed. Patients learn (if they don't already know) that obedience and often silence are appropriate patient demeanors, and that noisiness, anger, emotional outbursts, lateness (for whatever reason), and ingratitude (regardless of how one is treated) are viewed as unacceptable, even vulgar, disruptions of the medical social order. Of course such medical decorum is established and maintained by doctors, certainly not patients. Waitzkin (1991) further points out how class-based sociolinguistic differences between doctors and patients are manifested in doctor–patient relationships; how, for example, working-class patients are less likely to take verbal initiative when talking to their doctors, or to disagree with them.

bell hooks (1994a) describes one of her early realizations that "class was much more than one's economic standing, that it determined values, standpoint, and interests. . . . Those of us from diverse ethnic/racial backgrounds learned that no aspect of our vernacular culture could be voiced in elite settings . . . [we were] always in the position of interloper" (p. 182). Yet, even as medical students are trained in multicultural "sensitivity," they are routinely taught a monolithic mode of doctor–patient interaction based on middle-class, Western values: Patients should show appropriate deference to the physician's knowledge; they should be neat, clean, and punctual; and they should be willing to disclose very personal things about themselves. Patients who do not reflect this conception are difficult patients or "poor historians."

History Taking and Essentialism

While most physicians generally recognize history taking as the most important diagnostic tool in medicine (Coulehan, 1992; Pellegrino, 1980), today American medical practice is more concerned with the things of procedures, lab findings, organs, and cells. Narratives, that is, patients' stories, often come last.

One of the first clinical skills that medical students learn is how to listen to patients in order to reproduce their stories for the medical record. Students quickly learn that the doctor is author/authority in the creation of this historical document. Doctors decide what questions to ask within a received format and what words patients use are significant enough to include in the record. This makes it not a *history* per se or even a *record*, which implies a correspondence between events that exist "out there" and what the doctor actually records on the page. Perhaps the document should be called the *doctor's* record of the patient, not *the* medical record, which suggests a more inclusive authorial voice. Indeed, the overprivileged status of physicians, coupled with their denial of the advantages they gain from patients' lesser authority and lack of clinical knowledge, protects physicians' privilege from being fully acknowledged, lessened, or ended.[5] Moreover, medical education gives no training in helping doctors see themselves as "unfairly advantaged, or as . . . participant[s] in a damaged culture" (Macintosh, 1993, p. 210). Quite the opposite: Doctors are schooled to think of themselves as altruistic, caring healers (which most are), and the culture in which they live and work reinforces these beliefs by highly positioning doctors socially and economically. Doctors are the subjects acting upon and for the patients as objects. Doctors are Us, patients are Other. Yet doctors didn't just ascend to this position on their own at this historical moment; Walker Percy wrote unceasingly in his essays and novels about the "layman's canonization of science, which the latter never asked for" (1971, p. 7).

Thus the synergy resulting in the reproduction of physicians' social privilege originates from inside and outside the profession. Viewed from this perspective, doctor–patient encounters become what Waitzkin (1991) calls "micropolitical situations" that "reflect and support broader social relations, including social class and political-economic power" (p. 9). In spite of the increased proportion of underrepresented minorities and women in medicine, only 12% of U.S. medical students come from working-class families, a figure that has remained unchanged since 1920 (p. 22). Thus the comfortable lifestyle of most physicians, whether derived from their families of origin or their newly acquired social position, may inhibit them from criticizing or actively working against oppression brought about by the very class structure that grants physicians social and economic privileges. As Waitzkin reminds us, when physicians fail to confront or criticize the social context of the problems patients bring to the medical encounter, they implicitly or explicitly reproduce the dominant ideology that may be the source of their patients' suffering.

ESSENTIALISM AND WHITENESS IN THE MEDICAL ACADEMY

A Curriculum Example

I had 15 students in my class "Girls to Women: Coming-of-Age Narratives in Literature." They were a mix of second-, third-, and fourth-year medical students; our racial/ethnic/national origins were in Europe, Asia and the Middle East, Africa; half were women. Before we even met in class, I put the following statement at the top of their syllabus, which was available for all students to peruse before signing up for classes: "PLEASE NOTE: This class is designed SPECIFICALLY to examine coming of age in fictions written across race, culture, and sexual orientation. Because white, middle-class, heterosexual orientations are so often presumed to be the 'norm' against which all other narratives are judged, I have selected authors/texts that focus on individuals who are African-American, Latina, and Chinese-American; several narrative voices are lesbian." These 15 students signed up because of this dictum, in spite of it, or oblivious to its possible meanings.

As I look back on that month-long class and my intentions so stated, I see it differently now. I believe that I made racist assumptions regarding essentialism from my position of privileged authority; here, *white* professor. Actually, I see irony everywhere (invisible as it was at the time). I was so intent on interrogating essentialist thinking by (seemingly) moving our focus away from whiteness as the locus of normality that critical questions regarding essentialism remained unasked. What were the overt and subtle ways essentialism was expressed in the texts we read? Were there any benefits from expressions of essentialist thought in any of the texts? How might these essentialist beliefs work against those on whom the expression was made? What essentialist beliefs might the characters in any of the texts have regarding white people? Were there any expressed? By not asking such questions, I implied that essentialism and its attendant risks and benefits apply only to marginal others, thus reinforcing the belief that "they" can be codified and that "they" are the ones keeping out those who are not like them. Yet white people also employ the politics of essentialist exclusion, but the difference, bell hooks reminds us, is that ours is often "firmly buttressed by institutionalized structures of domination that do not critique or check it" (1994a, p. 83). That is, no one seems to want to assert that dominant groups—men, white people, heterosexuals—perpetuate essentialism all the time as a means of maintaining identity or as a strategy for exclusion. Whiteness becomes the implicit standard in difference and diversity efforts:

It is striking that under the surface of sometimes sophisticated scholarly analysis and description of other races, peoples, or groups, both in earlier times and today, we find a powerful ideological layer of self-interest, in-group favoritism, and ethnocentrism. Whether the accounts are historical, ethnographic, psychological, sociological, political, economic, or cultural, many tend to focus on differences and not on similarities, on hierarchy and not on equality, on oppositions and not on variation, and a variety of corresponding metaphors that signal opposition and hierarchy, such as modern versus backward, fast versus slow, or efficient versus inefficient. (van Dijk, 1993, pp. 160–161)

In the context of my class, I used these literary texts as extraordinary exemplars of "not white" without critically confronting issues of race, power, and identity in those texts, in the class itself, and in the medical school and hospitals where they were receiving their training.

What I did may have been little more than provide a racialized smorgasbord, or worse yet, take students on what hooks calls the "jungle safari" (1994b, p. 5). This is the multiculturalist ideology Roman calls *difference as pluralism*, which is not what I intended in my class. Even though there was a total absence of "'white' coming-of-age narratives, an unspoken insinuation of the class was that white culture is the *hidden norm* against which all other racially subordinate groups' so-called 'differences' are measured" (Roman, 1993, p. 71). By selecting authors/texts representing marginalized groups only—"see how different we all are!"—I nonetheless set up that very fictitious white standard from which to read color. Even as we recognized that *of course* Celie's coming-of-age story in *The Color Purple* (A. Walker, 1982) doesn't parallel the stories of most African American women any more than the adolescence lived by the Garcia sisters, newly uprooted from the Dominican Republic to New York City in *How the Garcia Girls Lost Their Accents* (Alvarez, 1992), mirrors "the" immigrant experience, we managed to avoid confrontation with that ultimate control group we call white.

Hazards on the Multicultural Highway

Cameron McCarthy (1993) critiques most pluralist approaches to multiculturalism and questions the expectation that negative white opinions toward minorities will be altered if prejudiced individuals are given sensitivity training in human relations and "diversity," what Gloria Yamato (1990) calls the "one hellifying workshop" approach to eliminating racism (p. 20). McCarthy contends that trying to reverse the values, attitudes, and human nature of *individuals* without the conceptualization and critique of *institutions* as sites of power and the reproduction of existing

social arrangements does not create sufficient theories of or solutions to
the issue of racial inequality. That is, it is time to stop thinking of racism
as individual prejudice and start thinking of it in more structural and
politicized terms (Donald & Rattansi, 1992, p. 3). Moreover, what is
needed at multiple locations in the medical curriculum is "a political and
ethical principle of positive social justice . . . [that would] privilege the
human interests of the least advantaged . . . moving us beyond the 'be-
nign' pluralism and cultural relativism that is now embodied in certain
innocuous forms of multicultural education," one that "tolerates the existence of salsa . . . even enjoys Mexican restaurants, but . . . bans Spanish
as a medium of instruction" (Lloyd, quoted in McCarthy, 1993, p. 300).
What this means—I think—is that my class might be just fine without a
"white" coming-of-age text but is unacceptable without a critical reading
that locates whatever stories we *do* read in a culture that systematically
privileges and empowers whiteness.

I am not alone; elsewhere in the curriculum are many other sites that
reproduce race, class, and gender bias. It can be found in lectures, readings, and syllabi that may go as far as pointing out absences and exclusions of certain groups instead of *including* the work of those very groups,
whereby observing exclusions often counts as evidence of "sufficient inclusion." Or it can be found in academic tokenism, what Gloria Anzaldua
(1990) calls the "vampirism of colonized and indigenous" people under
the guise of diversity/multiculturalism (p. xxii). Or it can be found in
classes dealing with sexual "alternatives" that meet on Saturdays: not just
the day of the week, but the very word *alternatives* implies a degeneration
from the mean, a lapse in the order of things, a quirk to be attended to
even if it means ghettoizing it from the rest of the curriculum.

So what do I "do" with the fact of and construction of my whiteness
as I go about my life's work with an explicit antiracist pedagogical and
research commitment? Ignore it? Focus on it? hooks (1994a) writes about
"white women who have yet to get a critical handle on the meaning of
'whiteness' in their lives, the representation of whiteness in their literature, or the white supremacy that shapes their social status" (p. 104). Yet
even talking about white supremacy as a white women is charged with
potentially guilt-inducing meanings, a guilt that Adrienne Rich (1978)
claims is so easily provoked that it can practically become a form of social
control, even a kind of solipsism. She writes that this kind of guilt can
become

> a preoccupation with our own feelings which prevents us from ever connect-
> ing with the experience of others. Guilt feelings paralyze, but paralysis can
> become a convenient means of remaining passive and instrumental. If I can-

not even approach you because I feel so much guilt towards you, I need never listen to what you have actually to say; I need never risk making common cause with you. (pp. 306–307)

Similarly, Gloria Yamoto (1990) talks about many white women's "morbid" fascination with their/our guilt, so much so that we are immobilized as we "sit and ponder our guilt and hope nobody notices how awful [we] are. Meanwhile, racism picks up momentum and keeps on keepin' on" (p. 21). Or sometimes the guilt is manifested in "niceness," when whites who are well educated, well intentioned, and "generous of heart" actually perpetuate racism by "nicing" someone to death "with naiveté and lack of awareness of privilege" (p. 21).

I am more and more convinced that confronting one's privilege, whatever it might be, is a necessary dimension of working against unjust social relations. As a white person growing up in the United States, I saw how racism put those who were not white at a social and economic disadvantage, yet I never really thought much about how my white skin provided me with so many benefits: from knowing the dance expected of me by my well-educated, white interviewers who gave me my first academic appointment; to sharing similar social experiences with so many of my students; to not having to learn the implicit rules of institutions governed exclusively by other white, well-educated, economically privileged individuals; to having all my superiors, from deans to division directors to department chairs—all those who have a say in my academic status—share my skin color. Macintosh (1993) writes that "whites are carefully taught not to recognize white privilege, as males are taught not to recognize male privilege. . . . White privilege [is] an invisible package of unearned assets" (p. 210). Moreover, whites are taught to view themselves as normative and average, so that when we work to benefit others (as in the doctor–patient relationship, or any helping relationship), we see it as work which will let "them" be more like "us" (p. 210).

So intent have I been in *not* asking women of color for help, in *not* further inscribing what hooks calls a "servant–served" mentality by expecting them to help me conquer racism, that I have been paralyzed by the magnitude of unlearning my racism alone, by trying to recognize my "white female complicity . . . [and] the privileges white women receive in a racist structure" (hooks 1994a, p. 106). But how much learning and self-reflection and self-critique is "enough"? What does it mean to "unpack" my white privilege? I gave up the Horatio Alger myth long ago, and I try with limited consciousness to identify ways I move about the world in the favored circumstances my whiteness brings, all of which is conferred on me strictly by the luck of my birth. Translating these emerging, always unfinished awarenesses into activism in the dailiness of my teaching, writing, interacting with colleagues, serving on committees: There's the rub. Partly, I think, it is my own fear of making mistakes, letting it show, or appearing naive that keeps me from trying to build solidarity and coalitions with persons of color working from antiracist standpoints. Akin to the suspicion that some men encounter when working with women against sexism ("and just what's *their* agenda?" I often wonder), I worry about what Yamoto (1990) calls self-righteous racism: those who assign themselves as the "good whites," as opposed to the "bad whites," the former

> often so busy telling people of color what the issues in the Black, Asian, Indian, Latino/a communities should be that they don't have time to deal with their errant sisters and brothers in the white community. Which means that people of color are still left to deal with what the "good whites" don't want to . . . racism. (p. 21)

More morbid guilt, this time laced with a preoccupation with mastering *all* the information/answers so as not to lose face.

So what many of us have done to protect our ignorance in academic settings (in our writing, paper presentations, and so on) is to offer the obligatory, "mind numbing recitation of race/class/gender/sexual preference/age/ethnicity/ability/weight/dry-cleaning fluid allergy [that] often seems to substitute both for serious thought and for serious political action" (Sternhell, 1994, p. 2). But where did this academic ritual start? For me, I came to believe that explaining up front in my writing that I am white, middle-class, and heterosexual somehow says it all, explains everything. My confession is complete; exposing myself publicly is penance; I feel relieved that readers know that I have reflected so deeply that I can actually name my gender, race, social class, and sexual desires, and have an idea that these somehow influence what and how I think, teach, inquire, and write. The true locus of my inquiry now shifts to Others as I continue my attempt to "master" the subject of race and racism (hooks, 1994a).

Lous Heshusius (1994) questions this academic obsession with somehow "managing" our subjectivities and how we try to be in charge of it, handle it, restrain it, and account for it, as grounded in the belief that there is a possibility of a "regulated distance between self and other" (p. 15). As a white woman with an antiracist commitment in my teaching and research, when I identify my whiteness I have assumed that such explication (1) excuses any lapses, omissions, or covert racism and (2) is based on the belief that I can actually distance myself from my knowing and regulate that distance (p. 16). Heshusius questions such beliefs, suggesting that as teachers and researchers committed to social change we should be striving for a mode of consciousness, a way of being in the world that "requires an attitude of profound openness and receptivity," where one is "turned toward other (human or nonhuman) *without* being in need of it or wanting to appropriate it to achieve something" (p. 16).

Now I know that much of my never-ending task of unlearning my racism will be difficult, much of it solo, and will involve far more than rhetorical gimmickry. It will involve reading, thinking, watching myself and others; more reading, more thinking. But all this must eventually go somewhere as I learn to speak up and take a stand in ways that are not exploitative or oppressive.

ON RISING AND CONVERGING AGAINST RACISM

Those of us in the medical academy, whatever we happen to be doing— teaching, taking care of patients, administering, recruiting, advising— can take action to work against racism. For me, this is how it looks for now.

First, I refuse to take part in diversity/multicultural efforts that fall exclusively into a checklist mentality. Memorizing "traits" or "characteristics" of groups and equating that with "sensitivity" is a superficial, often racist approach that still retains hidden white, middle-class norms. Of course it is important for students to know that some groups bound by certain customs and beliefs may, for example, have clothing or other garments that may require more time for undressing or dressing than does Western dress. Of course it is important for students to know that some groups of women may be extraordinarily deferential to the authority of a male physician (or any physician) and may need extra time or different approaches during history taking and physicals than other women. But these understandings cannot be equated with the need for physicians to be acutely aware of the unique personal and social conditions that patients bring with them to the doctor's office, conditions that cannot be neatly codified or essentialized by race, ethnic group, age, or other identities.

Second, I continue to seek understandings of difference in ways that move in more than one direction, that is, Us (white) becoming more sensitive to Their (not-white) differences. Explicit in all our "diversity" attempts should be critical examination of (1) the values, commitments, and practices of the medical academy in all its educative efforts and (2) the implicit white norms found everywhere there. To ignore either of these is to "redouble" [their] superiority by "naturalizing" them (Fusco in Wallace, 1993). Medical students should be asked regularly to engage in a more systematic critique of the medical environment in which they are being absorbed—doctor's offices, clinics, hospitals—so that they can identify and critique the values these medical cultures embody, enact, expect. Somewhere in this multicultural morass we need to create a wider field of inquiry that includes the intersection of often disparate beliefs, expectations, and behaviors of doctors, patients, medical bureaucracies, government, and the insurance industry. Now, it seems, we are content to turn our gaze only on those outside the health care delivery system, mostly patients; size them up for "differences" (from us); then include these traits in syllabi, lectures, or practicums, hoping students' "sensitivity to diversity" will kick in when they encounter someone unlike themselves.

But what would happen if we were to begin our multicultural inquiry with critical questions aimed at the white, Westernized, capitalized, medicalized norms of the culture of health care delivery? How do these norms work on behalf of doctors? Patients? How do these norms work against doctors? Patients? How do those of us within the medical culture essentialize patients? How do we essentialize ourselves? As insiders, how do we assess the system in which we work, in which we have been socialized? Should we, and how should we, critique the social conditions in which patients live? What do we do with our realization that medical knowledge is "socially-produced, deeply imbued with human interests, and deeply implicated in unequal social relations" outside the office, hospital, or clinic (McCarthy, 1993, p. 295)? Van Dijk (1993) suggests that we become consistently and consciously antiracist in our approaches, which is different from being *for* something, such as multiculturalism. That is, "there is a rather crucial difference between strategically saying that one 'is of course against racism,' on the one hand, and consistently supporting anti-racist positions and policies, on the other hand" (p. 19).

I think of the ongoing tensions in my own professional life that have to do with if and how I confront unwarranted, even outrageous treatment I have received or witnessed along gender lines, and how often I accept it silently as part of the price of getting along. Derrick Bell (1994) describes this phenomenon:

> When considering how to respond to abuse in the workplace, it is all too easy to magnify the risks of confronting the abuser while diminishing the possibility that a strong response will either end the abuse or provide the satisfaction of having made clear that abusive behavior is unacceptable. (pp. x–xi)

This describes the pattern so well: I keep my mouth shut here (or there, again and again) to make my chances better for this promotion or to be selected for that award, while patterns of institutionalized abuse keep on in their monotonous, unchallenged, even unquestioned course.

Third, where do our efforts take place? Literally, of course, in the classroom. But where else might this be enacted in the vast medical culture in the United States? What about our writing and research? hooks (1992) reminds us that we can make conscious decisions about both our methods and our audiences, and she suggests the importance of writing "in a manner accessible to a broad reading public" even though it is often delegitimized in academic settings. She believes that one of the uses of theory in the academy is to produce and maintain "an intellectual class hierarchy" where the only work worthy of being called theoretical (and thereby valued) is "abstract, jargonistic, difficult to read, and containing obscure references. It is easy to imagine different locations, spaces outside academic exchange, where such theory would not only be seen as useless, but would be seen as politically nonprogressive" (p. 80). We can find these locations, hooks tells us, when we "move out of the academy and into the streets" (p. 80), not as exclusive discursive sites but as locations of collaborative theorizing and action.

Still, even as we recognize our privilege in the medical academy, problematize our essentialist thinking and other biases (those known to us, anyway), and recognize the paternalism, even hubris, of "Us doing for Them" in our commitment to work against oppressive social arrangements, we still teach, write, do research, and get promoted and tenured in that very environment. Indeed, "to be heard in the halls of High Theory, one must speak in the language of those who live there" (Lather, 1994, p. 184).

But what hooks proposes, and what I want to advance here, is to thread all our efforts—whatever our methods, wherever they may enacted—with a spirit of emancipation, partialness, and self-critique, and with a receptivity to others that displaces postures of expert knowledge and essentialist thought that dictate normality. To "go beyond rhetoric or evasion into that place in ourselves, to feel the force of all we have been trying—without success—to skim across" (Rich, 1978, p. 310). To think about what we're doing, to what end, to whose benefit.

7

Border Crossings in Medical Education

> Boundary crossing, from safe circle into wilderness: the testing of bound-
> ary, the consecration of sacrilege. It is the willingness to spoil a good party
> and break an encompassing circle, to travel from the safe to the unsafe. . . .
> To know that everything has changed and yet that nothing has changed.
> —Patricia J. Williams, *The Alchemy of Race and Rights*

BORDER: *margin, edge, brink, rim, brim.* Simply, the line that separates two things. Some of these lines are enormously useful, as when a mother says protectively to her child, "Now don't you go out of your yard." Or when a zoning board protects citizens' safety and aesthetic sensibilities by not allowing oil drilling within such-and-such a distance from their homes. Or when guidelines are established to distinguish between health and illness, as in "borderline hypertension."

Yet borders also promote insistent hierarchies, ethnocentrism, smugness, and other configurations of power, as in the palpable distinction between "scientific" and "not scientific," the former usually being perceived as the good stuff. Henry Giroux (1992), who has written extensively on the subject of borders, border crossings, and border pedagogy, believes that the category of *border* sets in motion an acknowledgment of those "epistemological, political, cultural, and social margins that structure the language of history, power, and difference" (p. 28). Border *crossings* signal ways existing boundaries shaped by domination, authority, and control can be challenged and redefined. Border *pedagogy* makes apparent the "historically and socially constructed strengths and limitations of those places and borders we inherit" that frame our thinking and the way we relate to each other (p. 28).

This, then, is my intention in the following pages of this chapter: to identify and cross over (some of) the borders in and around medical education, and to question the practices I find there.

IN THE CURRICULUM: THE TWO CULTURES REDUX

The number 2 is a very dangerous number: that is why the dialectic is a dangerous process. Attempts to divide anything into two ought to be regarded with much suspicion.

—C. P. Snow, *The Two Cultures*

Outside the ghettoization of the disciplines lies the possibility of creating new languages and social practices that connect rather than separate education and cultural work from every day life.

—Henry Giroux, *Border Crossings: Cultural Workers and the Politics of Education*

The atrophy of one's imagination begins with a medical student's earliest immersion in medicine. With great uniformity, medical students begin their medical studies in the basic sciences, an intense foray into facts, concepts, systems, stages, hierarchies. Sometime during their first or second year they begin human contact when they learn the skills of history taking, a ritualistic, formulized set of questions and postures that they use first with simulated patients, then with real ones. The knowledge and skills they acquire about the human body are understandably, yet oddly, abstract. That is, they learn little about an individual's contextual life, about the lived experience of being sick, despite admonitions about the attention they should give to individual human differences. Students then spend the last two years of their medical education cycling through the various specialties: internal medicine, surgery, pediatrics, and so on. The importance of role modeling is critical here: They watch, follow, listen, learn procedures.

Dualisms are deeply inscribed from the start in the language of medical discourse, in texts, during rounds and noon conferences, and in informal consultations; science (largely writ), objectivity, reason, distance, and doctors always end up on top. These dualisms also preserve the distance between the privileged I and the less entitled, sometimes ignored They, or Other.

With all that said, it is easy to see why humanities coursework in the midst of medical training has been seen somewhat as a renegade project. I think of it as such and ground my teaching in literature and medicine in several assumptions about the kind of classroom I have and always work toward. I believe my classes to be places for students to speak, think out loud, talk back, self-disclose, and articulate multiple, often contradictory, positions. I believe my classes to be places for all of us to engage critically with a subject (literature) and reflexively with our practices in light of, yet independent of, the literature. I believe that the content and methods of the humanities—literature in particular—are rich, complicated, provocative sources of exploration into the multiple and conflicting practices of health care. I believe that literary inquiry in medical education can be a place where personal vulnerability is invited, where students can openly confront the unspoken but everyday hurdles faced by doctors, what Robert Coles described as "our inevitably flawed humanity, our times of bitterness or envy or frustration or greed, our passions and dreams, our sometimes extravagant hopes and eager expectations, and . . . our moments of disappointment and melancholy" (1986, p. 2126). I believe literature provides stories of imaginary people in their everydayness that may lead readers toward empathically identifying with real people. I, along with others in the medical humanities, think that *our* disciplines are an especially good place to do such knotty, imaginative, intellectual work.

Yet, if I believe all these things about literature and my pedagogical practices surrounding it, I find myself in a position that causes some disturbances in the field of my own thinking. That is, when I ask students to read literature with the intention of confronting medical practices, I'm really asking them to be thoughtfully suspicious of a few of the venerable, taken-for-granted stations of science—objectivity, distance, and reason— and how these work, and don't work, in the complicated, multilayered, nuanced care of human beings. If such critical reflection on one's practice is really so important, shouldn't I, too, take a harder look at the assumptions I make about the medical humanities that guide my practice in the classroom and in the larger medical humanities discourse? Shouldn't I be thoughtfully suspicious of *my* disciplinary corrals as well?

Regarding our theorizing in the medical humanities, our ways of being with our academic kin and others attempting interdisciplinary humanities work in medicine, I need to ask: Who do we say we are? What do we say we do? Where do we position ourselves in medicine? What is the nature of our highly particularized discourse? How have we managed to reinforce predictable academic patterns of disciplinary-bound exclusions? How have we enacted that which we supposedly went into medical education to work against? I find several examples in my own teaching that give me pause. Here's one:

After many years of teaching literature and medicine, I find that I often slip unreflexively into a kind of literary evangelism that really makes me complicitous with the existing hierarchical structures of medicine as I subtly replace one imperialistic form of inquiry with another. Because of my zealousness for the content and methods of literary inquiry that may move students to adopt a more empathic practice, I run the risk of posing as Foucault's Grand Theorist, the "master of truth and justice" (1977, p. 12), literature and medicine-style. Those of us engaged in a critical analysis of medicine using literature (or any humanities discipline) may unwittingly position ourselves and our disciplines as possessing some kind of special knowledge that is more valid or trustworthy for such an analysis, one that may lead to better care of the *person* who is ill.

In my own classes, for example, I see how easy it is to contribute to the prevailing dualisms in our culture at large, and most certainly in medicine—objective/subjective, rational/ irrational, cognition/emotion, acquired/intuitive—by hoisting the latter in each dyad to heights where, I implicitly claim, we can really examine what we do, think, and feel, something we are unable to do when engaged in the dailiness of "real" doctoring that is informed by the distancing language of reason. Such dualisms are, of course, absurd—as if any one of us, poet or doctor, thinks and lives that way (or could, or should). Such enthusiasm, I fear, can take the form of a smugness embedded in a kind of humanities mystique: Over there, in the basic and clinical sciences, is where you acquire skills and habits of doctoring (technique); over here, in the humanities, is where you look for meaning (a noble and lofty pursuit).

Yet C. P. Snow in his famous two cultures lecture (1959) pointed out how impoverished such a perspective is, how the humanities side of the two cultures operates "as though the scientific edifice was not, in its intellectual depth, complexity, and articulation, [one of] the most beautiful and wonderful collective work[s] of the mind of man [*sic*]" (p. 14). He likened it to being tone-deaf:

> As with the tone-deaf, they don't know what they miss. They give a pitying chuckle at the news of scientists who have never read a major work of English literature. They dismiss them as ignorant specialists. Yet their own ignorance and their own specialisation is just as startling. A good many times I have been at gatherings of people who, by the standards of the traditional culture, are thought highly educated and who have with considerable gusto been expressing their incredulity at the illiteracy of scientists. Once or twice I have been provoked and have asked the company of how many of them could describe the Second Law of Thermodynamics. The response was cold: it was also negative. Yet I was asking something which is about the scientific equivalent of: *Have you read a work of Shakespeare's?* (p. 9)

This is to say two things. First, disciplinary hubris occurs everywhere. Of course. Second, a poem is not a necessary or sufficient organizer for creating the kind of classroom (or bedside teaching) where one's goal is to move students toward highly skilled, *empathic* medical care of *each* person, especially those least likely to receive such care. Teaching for this social practice, directly or by example, transcends disciplinary boundaries. I can think of many medical educators, including clinicians and basic scientists, who model and encourage this kind of critical awareness and imaginative projection into others' lives. There is the contemporary American geneticist Barbara McClintock, whose noninterventionist observation of patterns of growth in corn surely must have illuminated to students and colleagues the kind of deep respect for others—here, in nature—that we strive for in the content and methods of humanities inquiry in medicine. Or I think of physician Abraham Verghese (1994), as described in his memoir *My Own Country*, sitting on the porch of Vicki and Clyde McCrae's trailer in east Tennessee during a home visit to HIV-infected Clyde, sharing a forbidden cigarette with Vicki, soaking in the sun and light, quietly trading stories. What did the example of his life say to students rotating through infectious disease at the teaching hospital where he saw patients? What did the example of his life say to readers of his book?

All this is to say that empathy, which most surely involves the imagination as we try to feel what it is like to be *this* person "who has a life, a mode of thinking and feeling and seeing and listening and responding that are no one else's" (Coles, 1986, p. 2125), cannot be taught directly the way many medical skills and techniques can be, and that these qualities are by no means strictly in the province of the humanities.[1] Basic and clinical sciences *are* different domains of knowledge, with different protocols and cognitive styles from the humanities. Yet the questions embedded in these scientific disciplines, plus basic scientists' and clinicians' inquiry in labs, at the bedside, or behind the podium can be indistinguishable from the questions and styles of humanities inquiry in medical education.

Together, all of us who labor to educate future doctors can work against becoming the bearer of disciplinary/professional elitism in whatever we teach. When we no longer expect a kind of predetermined, "correct," informed enlightenment back from our students, we can "wander uncharted territory . . . aware [that] there are co-wanderers" (Joycechild in Lather, 1991, 128). Co-wandering in the land of medical education, a visionary land with more permeable borders, perhaps we can begin to ask as many questions as we (try to) answer, to look further than our own narrow specializations in our quests, and to recognize how one's imagination can be an important source of connection to patients.

IN THE CLINIC: ON (RE)LEARNING LANGUAGES

> We are all sitting on one side of the compartment or the other; we are all
> subject to the blindness imposed by our seats in the compartment; there is
> no other way of being on the train(chain).
> —Madan Sarup, *Post-structuralism and Postmodernism*

Monica is a fourth-year medical student, and this is her first week on her
family practice rotation. With their permission, she gets to meet patients
before the "real" doctor comes into the examining room. Standing outside the door, she examines the chart of Miranda, an 8-year-old girl whose
mother is fearful that the child's paternal grandfather may be sexually
abusing her. Inside the examining room, Monica does what every well-
trained medical student does and performs a skillful exam using the following format: chief complaint, history of present illness, past medical
history, social history, review of systems, tests ordered and results, assess-
ment of problem, treatment, and outcome.

But she needs more than her training has provided for her to become
the kind of doctor *she* aspires to be, which is more than a test score on a
clinical competency exam can ever say about her. She needs access to her
patients' lives outside of medical walls, in a language that is not distilled
to fit medical formats. Yet what she sees before her in the medical record
and what she participates in now as she records her own findings is the
translation of the patient's words and experiences (here, the mother's) into
the language of medicine and the creation of a product that can be pro-
cessed by a medical system.

What is missing in these written accounts, the spontaneous yet se-
verely prescriptive format of the chart, authored by the doctor, those first
words to hit the page that become The Story (in contradistinction to the
patient's lived experience of The Story), newly clinicalized, sterilized, pathologized? Rewritten, with doctors' pens; retold, in doctors' language,
always at a distance from the patient's actual experience. Indeed, as
Suzanne Poirier and Daniel Brauner (1988) point out, the physician mani-
pulates the patient's story by asking certain questions and arranging information to conform to the appearance, organization, and tone of
the medical report. And each time other caregivers get possession of the
record, ask more questions, record more information in their words,
the patient's story is further abstracted from

> experience that brings [her], voluntarily or not, to the physician. Distinguish-
> ing between these two events, one centered in the consciousness of the pa-
> tient and the other in the consciousness of the physician, raises an issue

central to the theory and practice of medicine: Is the story being told in the medical report the story of the patient's life or of the physician's relationship with the patient's illness? The tension between these two possibilities is a frequent factor in various ethical dilemmas. (p. 5)

Admittedly, history taking and the written medical record are practices that have served many people (doctors *and* patients) well for many years and could continue unproblematized. Thus this is a call not to revolutionize the chart but to probe some of the spoken and unspoken assumptions underlying medical discourse, an inquiry that may enhance the care doctors provide to patients by deepening their understanding of and respect for their patients.

I will address two problems arising from the conventions of the medical record. Poirier and Brauner illustrate the first by an example they witnessed during an interdisciplinary conference in geriatrics and gerontology. Once a week, interns were required to present one of their patients to the conference. Even though they were not given any particular format for their presentation, they invariably resorted to the traditional format they were taught during their second year of medical school. Their delivery was also predictable:

face and voice become expressionless, speech is usually either gently deliverable or rapidly businesslike. The patient is seldom named. The intern . . . uses passive verbs to avoid first person direct references to him or herself . . . is clearly reciting from the patient's medical record, and the "genre" has dictated the language, structure, and even tone of the oral presentation. (Poirier & Brauner, 1988, p. 6)

The patient is seldom named. The patient's illness and the responses to the illness, yes; but the fully human patient, someone's wife, daughter, mother, and friend, who has a lifetime of experiences and accomplishments, is not the stuff of the medical record, nor was it ever intended to be. But a top-notch doctor is aware of these limitations, recognizes what has been omitted in the medical record, and knows that behind the chart's language is a fully lived human life. Right? Perhaps, but the chart's tone of authority and anonymity "may artificially absolve any feelings of doubt the physician may have . . . [and] discourage self reflection. The language and form of the medical case report can thus allow a physician to be unaware of her or his own feelings or values" (Poirier & Brauner, p. 7).

The second related problem of the language of the medical record has to do with the way the format restricts imaginative thought, the tradeoff being the economical use of language that shears off (seemingly) extraneous details of a patient's life, the patient's "narrative," leading to a speedy, efficient resolution of whatever medical problem the patient has. History taking, usually the first clinical (and most important diagnostic) skill that medical students learn in medical school, is really learning to listen to and tightly reconstruct patients' narratives for the medical record. Yet Jack Coulehan (1992) calls the term *history taking* unfortunate phraseology, with the word *take* implying that it is something doctors "wrench" away from the patient, and the word *history* objectifying the story and implying that it is an established thing, "something we extract like a plane's black box from the wreckage of the person's life" (p. 361).

Indeed, when patients are discussed during grand rounds and other teaching conferences, it is often in terms of laboratory data. And when the story that the patient gives (the subjective, soft stuff) conflicts with the lab data (the objective hard stuff), the patient's story is often given less credibility; "it might well be ignored or minimized and the patient attacked for being a 'poor historian'" (Coulehan, 1992, p. 361). Yet it is the physician who is asking the questions and reconstructing the patient's words to fit into the format of the medical record. One very distinctive mark of being a poor historian—actually an unpardonable methodological flaw—is to ignore competing explanatory frames or to fail to acknowledge one's theoretical standpoints. Perhaps, Coulehan suggests, the physician is the poor historian?

I propose that what is missing here is the imagination. The doctor's, that is.

IN THE IMAGINATION: TOWARD A MORE EMPATHIC PRACTICE OF MEDICINE

> Literature is the lie that tells the truth, that shows us human beings in pain and makes us love them, and does so in a spirit of honest revelation.
> —Dorothy Allison, *Skin*

I started this chapter lamenting how students begin to lose the capacity for imaginative thought when they enter medical school. But I've not really answered the question, "What does the imagination have to do with good doctoring, anyway?" Some possibilities:

The ability to image the life world of the patient—where and how the patient is in charge in all those waking moments outside the examining room or hospital bed—has a great deal to do with good doctoring. Yet, as I suggested earlier, medical practice often whittles away the subtleties and suggestions embedded in patients' language as it moves with increasing inductive precision toward classification and diagnosis. This is the nature of medical discourse as it is verbally enacted in history taking and as it is recorded with great economy of language in the formulized medical record; this is what Elliot Mishler (1984) calls the *voice of medicine*. This is because physicians are the active collectors and analyzers of technical information elicited from patients; comparatively, patients are passive. Almost all patients have no knowledge of what the physician is recording about them right before their very eyes. In fact, Mishler asserts that "only the physician's judgment of the relevance and significance of information is retained in the patient's record" and that "there are no external checks on possible distortions or misunderstandings of different perceptions by patients of what has been said or left unsaid" (1984, p. 10). Yet when patients attempt to interrupt the structure and content prescribed by the physician in the typical interview, an act Mishler calls the *voice of the patient*, physicians "rapidly repair such disruptions and reassert the voice of medicine" (Mishler, p. 95). Physicians' refocusing in such situations is an act of context stripping, which keeps them in a dominant position, implicitly downgrading the lived problems of patients.

There are several ways medical educators can work against this configuration of power, ways that involve enlarging rather than restricting the imaginative attention physicians give to the lives of patients. I cite the words of Joanne Trautmann Banks, who over 25 years ago put forth what is still the most eloquent argument for the inclusion of literature in the medical school curriculum. Hers is the most convincing response I can make to medical students who ask why they should read fiction in the midst of their medical training: "A fully imagined life is generally much more complete than our own" (Banks, 1982, p. 23). Through their training, medical students come to believe that reality presents itself empirically to them in some kind of systematic clinical way. But, as Banks argues, no matter how well developed one's observational skills are, they are never good enough to see the fullness of details in any given situation. Whose perceptual skills are, for that matter? Moreover, no one has the time or the ability (especially doctors in their constant barrage of rates, counts, and findings) to sort through what they perceive to be "extraneous" details in a meaningful way. More often than not most of us are not even aware of our surroundings; thus doctors' realization of "reality"—or, more importantly, their take on a patient's reality—is always biased, blurred, and partial. "We move through unseen worlds," says Banks (1982, p. 24), not because of any intention to do so, but because we come to look for only what is before us and what we want to see.

All professional discourse becomes more narrower, technical, abstract, and exclusionary with the increasing specialization of those who use it. Medical discourse is no different when it privileges a patient's disease in all its physiological complexities over other dimensions of that patient's life, thereby situating patients-as-their-illnesses. Thus not only do patients' lives outside medicine become the "unseen worlds" doctors move through, but doctors may sleepwalk through their own worlds, too, or, to use a previous metaphor, doctors may get stuck in cowpaths of their own and medicine's making even when some of the answers (and questions) lie outside these grooves. Literature, then, might not only enlarge one's understandings of others, it can—if we allow it—turn readers back on themselves to scrutinize their own beliefs and values.

So how does this relate to students in the midst of medical training? I return to Monica, the medical student whose patient, as it turns out, *had* been sexually abused by her grandfather. Monica wants to learn more about caring for this child and others like her. She turns to a respectable source, the AMA and its *Diagnostic and Treatment Guidelines on Child Sexual Abuse* (1992), to find the "views of scientific experts and reports in the scientific literature as of March 1992" (p. 5). (Note the word *scientific* is used twice; this is the *real deal* here.) Not surprisingly the table of contents contains such headers as "facts," "presentation," "findings," "physical examination," "documentation," and "risk management"; this is the language of medical discourse, and it is not intended or expected to be otherwise. But she also turns to a fictional account of child sexual abuse, Dorothy Allison's (1993) *Bastard Out of Carolina*, because she is searching for versions of abuse that may provide understandings to her that medicine cannot provide.

Consider the possible reader responses to the following medical and fictional passages on child sexual abuse. *MEDICINE* denotes the AMA guidelines cited above; *FICTION* denotes the voice of the patient, here in the narrative voice of 12-year-old Bone in *Bastard Out of Carolina*.

MEDICINE

Child sexual abuse can be defined as the engagement of a child in sexual activities for which the child is developmentally unprepared and cannot give informed consent. (p. 5)

FICTION

[The abuser, Daddy Glen, to Bone] "You think you're so grown up. You think you're so big and bad, saying no to me. Let's see how big you are, how grown!" His hands spread what was left of my blouse and ripped at the zipper on my pants, pulling them down my thighs as my left hand groped to hold them. I tried to kick, but I was pinned. Tears were streaming down my face, but I wasn't crying. I was cursing him. (p. 284)

MEDICINE

Survivors of child sexual abuse often experience long-term effects on their psychological and social well-being. (p. 5)

FICTION

Everything hurt me: my arm in its cotton sling; the memory of the nurse's careful fingers . . . my hip where it pressed against the mattress. Most of all my heart hurt me, a huge swollen obstruction in my chest. . . . Every time I closed my eyes there was a flash of Glen's face as he had looked above me. . . . I wanted my life back, my mama, but I knew I would never have that. (pp. 302, 307)

Both accounts are complex, limited rhetorical strategies. The voice of medicine is neutral, matter of fact, businesslike. It contains facts that the doctor–reader absorbs, from demographics to the physicians' proper behavior ("objective and nonjudgmental"). Like other nonfictional accounts of illness, this language "tells" readers what this or that is. It speaks in terms of appropriate, that is *universalizable*, developmental terms. It abstracts a child's pain to "long-term effects" and such vague descriptors as "social well-being." This language sounds like

the dispatches of war correspondents. While they describe in considerable detail the way [illness] attacks and how the campaign against it works, they don't go much beyond this. They tell the reader a lot about the waking life of the . . . patient, but not much about his daydreams or fantasies, about how illness transfigures you. You wouldn't know from them that inside every seriously ill person there's a Kafka character . . . trying to get out. (Broyard, 1990, p. 1)

Or inside a sexually abused 12-year-old there's a girl named Bone trying to get out.

The voice of fiction, here in the voice of a patient, bids the reader to take an imaginative leap into another world. According to Italo Calvino (1986), literature "gives voice to whatever is without a voice . . . [to] aspects, situations, and languages both of the outer and of the inner world" (pp. 98–99). This is the victim's inner world at the moment of violence, exposing a child's solitary, raw terror at the hands of her raging stepfather. The author of this fiction achieves this not by using voyeuristic gimmicks focusing on crude sexual details, or by citing physical and psychological manifestations of sexual abuse, but rather by using language that encourages intersubjectivity between the reader and Bone's *experience* of the violence. Indeed, Dorothy Allison herself admits that "when I sit down to make my stories, I know very well that I want to take the reader by the throat, break her heart, and heal it again" (1994, p. 180). And how well she succeeds here.

The voice of medicine, in contrast, tends to strengthen itself; when it attempts to portray the voice of the patient, it is usually done through *medical* screens and protocols using medicalized, psychologized signifiers. Fiction is not limited in this way to medical decorum, but it is, Calvino (1986) tells us, "like an ear that can hear things beyond the understanding of the language of politics" (p. 98), here, beyond the language and understandings of medicine. Can medical discourse as it is currently enacted capture pain so deep that it makes a 12-year-old's "heart hurt . . . a huge swollen obstruction in [her] chest"? Fiction can. It has the ability to "impose patterns of language, of vision, of imagination, of mental effort, of the correlation of facts, and in short the creation . . . of a model of values that is at the same time aesthetic and ethical, essential to any plan of action" (Calvino, 1986, p. 99). The voice of medicine asks readers/ listeners to focus on illness; the voice of the patient, often startlingly portrayed in fiction, asks readers/listeners to use what Banks (1982) calls "that higher faculty that involves thought and feeling in a visionary way, the faculty we call imagination . . . [which is] a sort of leap" (p. 29).

Fiction, then, when read concurrently with medical discourse—border crossing at some of its best—may invite readers to dare such leaps, to connect imaginatively, and thus more empathically, with patients. It does so not by the use of directives, the how-to's, the look-for-this-not-that often found in the voice of medicine. Quite the contrary. Literature, according to Rushdie, "tells us there are no rules. It hands down no commandments. . . . And it tells us there are no answers; or, rather, it tells us that answers are easier to come by, and less reliable, than questions. . . . Literature, by asking extraordinary questions, opens new doors in our minds" (1990, p. 10).

The title of this chapter contains the word *border,* which I have referred to here as the constructed boundaries between science/medicine and literature. These crossings do not need to be struggles for authority; rather, they can be sites of imaginative collaboration, places to examine the partiality of knowledge and knowledge making, places to consider the best insights and methods of varied discourses.

As teachers engaged in the adventure of educating doctors, we can work toward honoring and teaching in these borderlands. We can do so by

challenging existing boundaries of knowledge and creating new ones . . .
to engage the multiple references that constitute different cultural codes,
experiences, and languages. This means educating students to both read
these codes historically and critically while simultaneously learning the limits of such codes, including the ones they use to construct their own narratives. (Giroux, 1992, p. 29)

And in doing so, we can rise to C. P. Snow's (1959) challenge after all, to
welcome the creative chances at the "clashing points of two subjects, two
disciplines, two cultures" (p. 16).

8

Coda: Three Significant Landscapes

Women's intellectual work in the university *is* of a different order than that of our Anglo-European male colleagues. Women, it still seems, are treading on foreign and often hostile territory of male domains, and therefore are caught up in political struggles which are quite different in kind from those men engage in among each other.

—Carmen Luke and Jennifer Gore,
Feminisms and Critical Pedagogy

If you want someone to tell it like it is, you have to hear it like it is.
Shulamitz Reinharz, quoted by Michelle Fine,
"Dis-stance and Other Stances"

IN THE PRECEDING pages of this book, my intentions were to write from a feminist standpoint, recognizing all the while that feminism has always been a shifting signifier with historical and cultural contingencies. As a white North American feminist working in the highly privileged space of a medical academy, I *do* have a particular view. This view I choose—to the extent that I "control" such choices—is one among many overlapping perspectives looking out on the world with a commitment to social change.

Similarly, in acknowledging that my theoretical allegiance to feminism commingles with others, I also recognize that there is no *one* authoritative narrative for social change. In fact, as Sleeter and McLaren put forth, "there must be multiple narratives as different groups of people define their own identities, analyze the circumstances of their oppression, and chart strategies for their empowerment" (1995, p. 11). Thus, even as I focus my feminist commitments on women in medicine as faculty, physicians, and patients, I work with others who share similar political goals of social change, even if they differ in how they theorize class, gender, race, and sexual practices. I do not view gender as the primary axis of oppression, nor do I propose that gender is a "theoretical variable separate from other axes of oppression. . . . Gender as a category of analysis cannot be abstracted from a particular context while other factors are held stable" (Alcoff & Potter, 1993, p. 3).

Thus feminism works toward ending unjust social relations found at the crossroads of various identities of which gender is but one. As such, I try to engage in a critical multicultural practice that cannot be reduced to method or manifesto but is, rather, a specific ideological stance that I forge with others as a way of living in and challenging the world critically, contesting inequitable power relations. Together we preferentially opt for particular attitudes and actions favoring the educationally, economically, and socially disenfranchised.

Power relations in the U.S. health care delivery system are, of course, ubiquitous. They negatively affect women, poor and uninsured people, uneducated people, persons who are not white, old people, non-English-speaking people (or merely the inarticulate), or anyone who is not a possessor of some kind of power, authority, or financial security. Such power relations exist in the academy, where gender and racial politics are still enacted within both faculty and student ranks; they clearly exist at the level of health care delivery. These relations can be overt responses (including disregard or inaction) that directly impinge on a person's health, or they can exist at the level of nuance—looking, or not looking; an extra moment, or one less; touching, or not touching—which also may influence a patient's health.

I close this book with more experiences, illustrating the lure of silences and scripts that help feminists survive in institutions built on militaristic configurations of power and authority; rigid, rationalist epistemological commitments; and a Darwinian approach to who gets what.

ON UNLEARNING RACISM

> No need to hear your voice when I can talk about you better than you can speak about yourself. No need to hear your voice. Only tell me about your pain. I want to know your story. And then I will tell it back to you in a new way. Tell it back to you in such a way that it has become mine, my own. Re-writing you, I write myself anew. I am still author, authority. I am still the colonizer, the speaking subject, and you are now at the center of my talk.
>
> —bell hooks, *Yearning: Race, Gender, and Cultural Politics*

I am in a meeting with a dozen colleagues. It is an important one—the academic tribunal for medical students who receive too many poor grades or who are experiencing "noncognitive" difficulties. I serve on this sometimes gut-wrenching committee to counter the (self-proclaimed) "hard asses" who are constantly poised to dismiss students. Numbers and test scores count here, big time: In this setting they are the primary index of whether or not a student has mastered the subject matter.

We're a fairly eclectic group: a few basic scientists, a few clinicians, a few administrators, a student representative; there are men and women who are racially diverse seated at the table. One member of the committee is our director of minority affairs: a fortyish African-American man; highly educated and credentialed; well-liked and respected by students, faculty, and administration; and "successful" by several important standards—his tireless work with the admissions office has brought about a significant increase in the number of African-American students enrolled at the college (a figure that had been one of the worst in the country in medical education), and he has worked hard to create a supportive environment for those students once they're in medical school. I like him very much, and we've talked often about our work, our frustrations, our successes.

We're on a break now between terrified students, standing outside the conference room. He has just told me of an opening in his three-person office. To date, all three persons have been African-American. I blurt out, "Well, maybe it's time to hire a white person in your office." He looks at me a bit puzzled, but we can't continue the conversation because just at that moment the committee chair calls us back in, and we return to our places at the table.

What I didn't get to tell him was my reasoning for this unsolicited advice, which was at once thoughtless, ill-informed, well-intentioned, and yes, racist. That is, I transposed my view, based at least in part on my membership in the dominant racial group in the institution, and assumed that it neatly matched his: that a white person in that office would somehow mean the institution took minority affairs more seriously, that the African-American minority affairs office would be better integrated, literally and symbolically, into the institution if there were a white person there. Or, since our institution has a pathetic hiring record for African-Americans (single digits here, with three in minority affairs), I thought that hiring a white person in that office would send a message to the institution that they could no longer hire African-Americans to work only in minority affairs or minority recruiting.

But what I had said nagged at me the rest of the day and on into the next. I knew I'd said something wrong but didn't know what. Then it finally dawned on me: How *dare* I suggest to him that he should hire a white person? I thought of Native American activist Mary Ritchie's (1995) observations about such behavior:

In the process of creating a multicultural discourse, people of color have
come to be the ingredients of the multicultural mix, which the dominant
culture is determining for us. . . . Our ideas and voices risk becoming blurred
and buried by constant attempts at understanding people of color from a
point of view which reifies a Eurocentric system and academic process of
domination. . . . We want a say in the outcome; we can speak for ourselves.
What needs to happen is that our voices not be usurped or interpreted by
our "benefactors." (1995, p. 310)

As the associate director of the Women in Medicine program at the medical school where I teach, I thought of how I would react if a *male* told me
I should hire a *male* to fill an opening in our program. I would be out-
raged. The arrogance of such thinking, that a program serving women
needed a man for institutional validation, represents the worst kind of
hubris of a dominant group to unproblematically determine what is
"best" for the nondominant group.

Yet I had done exactly the same with my suggestion to the minority
affairs director. In a later conversation we had, he informed me further
(kindly, thoughtfully) of how naive and ill informed my words really had
been. Quite simply, he was looking for someone to fill the position whom
minority students would feel comfortable with, trust, and seek advice
from in a medical environment that was indifferent to them at best, hostile at worst. I did not take into account what bell hooks describes as
critical to nondominant groups: *First* there must be the ability to "dialogue with one another, to give one another that subject-to-subject recognition that is an act of resistance that is part of the decolonizing, anti-
racist process" (hooks & West, 1991, p. 5).

Of course, committed allies from dominant groups *are* important to
struggles for social justice. The contemporary American psychiatrist and
medical educator Leah Dickstein has often called such allies "men of
good conscience" in women's labors for the equitable sharing of social,
economic, and political advantages. Lesbian, bisexual, and gay communities use the term *ally* to describe heterosexual persons who join their
struggle for fair and safe treatment in both private and public places. And
here in the United States, there is a history of white civil rights activists
who have joined with persons from nondominant racial groups to end
the hold racism has in our culture. In these struggles, however, some
difficult questions must repeatedly be asked: Who is determining the
concept of multiculturalism or diversity? Where are the beliefs, lived experiences, and strategies of nondominant people in these debates? Are
those of us from dominant groups determining everyone's roles? Are we
in the driver's seat of the "steam roller of multiculturalism" (Ritchie, p.
314)? How do we from dominant groups seem to turn discussions around

to us and our issues? Am I doing that here? In what ways do dominant groups expect persons from nondominant groups to educate us, make us feel comfortable with or proud of our efforts, assuage our guilt? How do we work toward social justice in ways that do not reproduce patterns of domination?

The questions persist.

ON MAKING SPECTACLES OF OURSELVES: OUTLAW EMOTIONS IN MEDICAL SETTINGS

Misogynist thought has commonly found a convenient self-justification for women's secondary social positions by containing them within bodies that are represented, even constructed, as frail, imperfect, unruly, and unreliable, subject to various intrusions which are not under conscious control.
—Elizabeth Grosz, *Volatile Bodies: Toward a Corporeal Feminism*

She had committed the deadly sin of crying in the hospital.[1] There she was, a third-year medical student, where patients were no longer abstractions but were there before her, fully human, where her teachers were no longer behind podiums but caring for patients at the bedside. And she cried not once, but several times, often during morning report or standing in the hall during medicine rounds when questioning often becomes confrontational, where pimping occurs, where what one does *not* know is laid bare before everyone to witness. Here is where she first cried, when a resident asked her a particularly obscure question that she could not answer. She cried because she was frustrated, because she felt insecure about her lack of knowledge, because she felt as though she were being ridiculed. Her behavior then and in subsequent tearful moments made everyone uncomfortable, annoyed a few, and upset her supervisors because they felt they could not offer even the most gentle feedback to help her increase her knowledge base and improve her clinical skills. The situation was brought to our attention by her clerkship director at the hospital; we read his concern as genuine and nonconfrontational.

During the meeting in the hospital to discuss Rebecca's "problem" (at which she was present), we learned much about her: her childhood on a farm in a southern state; her family's deep religious convictions, an orientation she still possessed; a childhood marked by rigidity and relentless criticism. She had been very successful in medical school, her only difficulty appearing in her second year when she was required to "perform" her first patient interview. Not possessing what her supervisors called well-developed "social skills," Rebecca found thinking on her feet in stressful situations very difficult, especially in the face of critical feedback. And now she was crying in the hospital, and the task before us was to figure out what to do with/to/for Rebecca.

Our group discussed Rebecca for a long time. We all recognized that there was a skilled doctor in the making here. But what should we recommend? Everyone agreed that we should find ways to help Rebecca learn how *not* to cry under these circumstances and to read her peers' and supervisors' analyses of her interactions with patients as supportive rather than overly harsh. Because she was already in the midst of ongoing psychological counseling that she reported as being helpful, we believed such counseling would eventually have a positive impact on her interactions with peers and faculty ("I'm learning the difference between constructive and destructive criticism," she reported to us). Thus, while additional therapy was not the answer, there was a push to do something, *anything* to stop the crying in the hospital. Crying is just not acceptable behavior in most workplace settings; one of the unwritten but stern codes of "professionalism" for physicians is the stance of *detached* concern. As one clinician pointed out, "They'll eat her up when she's in surgery." That they probably would.

But then came the bombshell from the chief resident who supervised Rebecca, a comment that embodied all the smug, hierarchical positioning and privilege that still find their way into the socialization of medical students into the profession: "Well someone should just tell her to get herself together 'cause pretty soon it's going to be sink or swim. . . . Someone needs to toughen her up . . . put her into hard situations right now before it's too late."

The speaker was a woman.

Why is this always so disheartening and still surprising, hearing an accomplished, highly respected woman advocating something so medically macho and Darwinian? Perhaps it is my wistful belief that women might bring a certain civility to these settings previously inhabited exclusively by men, with less jockeying for position and control and more mutuality and collegiality. More tolerance. A belief that as a historically subordinated group in medicine, women would dismantle the offensive rooms in the master's medical house without toppling the entire structure. That is, while women would embrace medical knowledge and methods that have provided so many of us with healthier lives than ever before, they would *reject* the enactments of power played out in most of the human encounters doctors have with patients, families, and all other health care providers—that is, with everyone who has less power and prestige than physicians. A hope that women in medicine might use their power in these relationships to subvert the very institutional and social asymmetry implicit in medicine so that *patients*, not always the authorizing/directive doctors, are the revolutionary actors of health care dramas (Fisher, 1993). Or that women in medicine might be less apt to buy into the mythological "ideal" of dispassionate caregiving.

But we are talking about medical education here, where women are not trained in a separate feminized track devoid of power-driven standards of distance, objectivity, and control (of both others and oneself), nor are they given encouragement or skill in recognizing, confronting, or changing such standards. All doctors in training are the receivers of medicalized codes of behavior, and these certainly do not include expressive, embodied vulnerability or tenderness in their interactions with peers, patients, or the public. Sink or swim, Rebecca.

Still, why do these traits prevail with increasing numbers of women in medicine and medical education? Critical mass has typically been defined as a strong minority of at least 15%; women in medicine are found in higher percentages everywhere except in the offices of deans, senior associate deans, department chairs, and a few clinical specialties. Large numbers of women are *everywhere*, women who only recently have been allowed equal access to entering the profession. Could it be that socialization is so powerful and profound that even now, critically massed, women in medicine assume a colonizing role themselves, participate in the surveillance and quality control of novices into the profession, and see that medicine makes a man out of every aspiring doctor?[2] Medical education, after all, catches everyone indiscriminately in social nets that have profound implications, many of which are written on the body. In the eyes of her teachers, Rebecca's body obviously needed lots of work.

Feminists have theorized the body in several ways, one of which has implications for Rebecca's body. This has to do with postmodern conceptions of the body as a surface without depth, what Elizabeth Grosz (1994) calls the pliable "raw matter" to be "inscribed and reinscribed by social norms, practices, and values" (p. 138). Such surfaces allow for bodies to be categorized into socially significant groups, such as male and female, black and white, young and old. But bodies are also inscribed through lifestyles, habits, and behaviors. What the body *does* effects a surface inscription—what it eats, if and how it exercises, how it dresses, moves, and responds to others. Through these, Grosz continues, "the body is more or less marked, constituted as an appropriate, or as the case may be, inappropriate body, for its cultural requirements" (p. 142).

This body is social and public; it is written upon or produced by myriad jurisdictions or regimes of institutional power as a certain *kind* of body. In medicine, the inscribed body of the physician, both male and female, is marked as decisive, objective, rational, and, above all, composed. The performances incised on medical students' bodies are from head to toe, including a forthright gaze, handshake, and stride, along with countless other nuanced ways of moving throughout the halls of medicine. Doctors *control* interviews, procedures, practices. Of course the doctor's body may touch or exhibit other caring gestures, facial expressions, or tender tones, but it is a body *in control* of itself.

Rebecca's crying was read, of course, as not being in control. Moreover, her behavior reinforced basic social divisions based on gender; her habitus—her bearing, movements, ways of speaking, thinking, acting, what Bourdieu (1977) calls "embodied history"—was coded as female, thus not male, thus not doctor-like, thus not professional.

However, it is interesting to note here that in her study of women surgeons, Joan Cassell observed interactions between women surgeons and patients, nurses, chiefs of surgery, colleagues, and residents where "feminine" behavior was encouraged and agonistic "masculine" behavior penalized. She tells the stories of two women who indicated that during their surgical training, a senior male physician had advised them to wear lipstick so that no one would think they were lesbians. Cassell (1996) writes:

> Women who possess the wrong body in the wrong place must not be "real" women to place themselves in that situation: hence the lipstick, as embodied refutation of not-woman status. The male mentors, who counsel the women to wear lipstick, also advise them on becoming proficient surgeons: the wrong body, yes, but the right place; the body can move, react, think, behave like a surgeon. Each half of the double accusation, wrong body, wrong place, must be rebutted. (p. 44)

Such corporeal regulation is deeply inscribed, but is a regulation that forces women to decide whether or not to wear such masks; to seek or accept "adoption" by a male superior as symbolic daughters; to challenge their physical, symbolic, and social subordination virtually throughout medical hierarchies; or to complain and risk being branded as whiny and not up to the challenge. It is no wonder, then, that women medical students must constantly ask themselves how to change their "wrong body": What kind of female body *is* a doctor's body? What does her body's surface already possess of the embodied ethos of this group or class we call doctors? What surfaces are plastic? What are the costs of such plasticity?

Rebecca was learning something important here: On her body there are to be no raw edges, no open wounds, and no excess of anything; this is the medicalized, masculinized body. Never mind that physicians participate in all that makes us human from birth to death; minister to all the mysteries and magic of the human body; and bear witness to others' joy, shame, guilt, fear, and pain: The doctor's performance must not falter. Toughen up, Rebecca; it's what your teachers demand right now.

For to become a doctor is to become detached and reasoned, and "not only has reason been contrasted with emotion . . . it has been associated with the mental, the cultural, the universal, the public, and the male, whereas emotion has been associated with the irrational, the physical, the natural, the particular, the private, and, of course, the female" (Jaggar, 1993, p. 115). Rebecca, by her embodied emotional response, was, in the eyes of her peers and supervisors, blocking her ability to "be" rational. The emotions are not merely inappropriate epistemic *sources* in medicine that exist in opposition to rationality, they are improper and disruptive *responses* in medical settings. Thus, by molding the emotional character of young physicians-in-training in particular ways, medicine helps to guarantee its own reproduction, its own scripts, its own masks. It does so not by coersive force; rather, "it surveys, supervises, observes, measures the body's behavior and interactions with others. . . . [And] it punishes those resistant to its rules and forms" (Grosz, 1994, p. 149). Rebecca's pliable and trainable body was perceived by her teachers as capable of being "tuned" to a more "professional" (read: distanced and controlled) performance. The dominant values implicit in such molding, however, regulate one's capacity for indignation and anger, so that Rebecca will probably eventually lose "the ability to image a world that is any different from that of the present" (Welch, 1990, p. 20).

What were the dominant values in operation in Rebecca's case when she inevitably experienced/displayed outlaw emotions? She was in a small-group setting in which sensitive feedback was provided ostensibly to help her communicate more effectively with patients. It was a rational, civilized exchange that supposedly had nothing to do with the gender of the sender or the receiver of the feedback . . . or did it? Cassell (1996) observed in her study of women surgeons that there is always "something profound, nonlogical and nonverbal, something embodied" going on in this medically macho milieu (p. 42). Crying is raw emotion, a body unable to control itself, "internality externalized" (p. 43). Nurses can do it, families and patients can do it, but doctors' ritualized socialization excludes this behavior and anything like it. Indeed, medical socialization

> sculpts social agents who, by internalizing and embodying the dominant modes of thought and experience inherent in [medicine], are relatively inflexible: they look, feel, and behave like members of their particular gender, class, and grouping. These social agents then transmit to the next generation the embodied ethos of their group or class. (p. 44)

The responses to Rebecca's crying—discomfort, annoyance, embarrassment—are understandable given this explanation, but they are not acceptable. Just as we would not force a student with an anxiety disorder to "toughen up" in stressful situations, we should consider nothing less than supportive patience and encouragement in helping Rebecca through this difficult dimension of her medical training. This would not include purging crying from her behavior—even her public doctor-behavior—but would include helping her work with peers and supervisors in ways that move toward increasing her self-confidence; accepting and learning from appropriate suggestions to improve her clinical skills; developing responses to undeserved criticism in ways that do not leave her drained. The revolutionary work of removing oppressive structures in medical education would seek ways to develop skills and attitudes in our doctors-in-training that are not always based on the received standards of an institution that thrives on hierarchical roles, rigidly defined spheres of practice, and circumscribed, disembodied responses to the care of humans at their most vulnerable. And like most revolutions, this feminist uprising begins with a local insurgency—here, in the dailiness of our lives, in the way we treat Rebecca.

ON HOPE

> The way things work
> is that eventually
> something catches.
> —Jorie Graham,
> "The Way Things
> Work"

Grace is an unlikely concept to find its way into these final pages. In its theological sense, grace is the freely given, unmerited favor and love of God that can be resisted or spurned but is always there if people allow themselves to be open to it. This text is hardly theological, yet I was struck with how the term characterized those times when my awareness of a student's spirit and passion to *know* unexpectedly overwhelms me. I am momentarily speechless, *present* to that student's yearning, aware of the gift that is before me in the short time I actually have with any of my students.

I return to the classroom for this third landscape, the site and source of my most joyful and difficult labors, the place over which all my theorizing hovers, becomes immersed, and circles back to again and again. This was the literature and medicine class I teach to fourth-year medical students; I return to our discussion of Dorothy Allison's *Bastard Out of Carolina* (1993). The class was pure pleasure, what those of us whose life projects are teaching can only hope for: reflective, challenging students; content we love; lively, provocative classroom exchanges. Fifteen senior medical students converged here in the last month of their medical education, and I was witness to their collective intelligence, inquisitiveness, and intensity.

My lecture notes matched the chronological organization of the novel, but I also wanted to discuss regional literature and southern literary traditions, particularly among women. In addition, I wanted to spend some time on the development of narrative voice, so critical to this novel. But such intentionality rarely proceeds smoothly, and the first comment out of a student's mouth as the class started was, "I can't believe she did it. *How* could she do it?" Nods and murmurs of agreement. They were referring to the end of the book when the narrator's mother, Anney, walks out of the life of her daughter, Bone, who had just been sexually assaulted by her stepfather, Daddy Glen, the very person with whom Anney was now leaving. This troubled students greatly, and they wanted to talk about it. No one wanted to believe that a mother would abandon her child under these circumstances, leaving with the very man who had so viciously harmed that child.

What can you say about a book that prompts such an intense emotional response in readers? What could students gain from reading a book so completely foreign to their own insulated, mostly middle-class childhoods, a book full of people whose lives were totally alien to what they envisioned for themselves? Why had I selected this book other than the fact that I was crazy about it—and haunted by it? To psychologize or medicalize a reason is easy: It is a book "about" a dysfunctional family or "about" child sexual abuse, phenomena medical students "need to confront." When the discussion first started, I began to question my motives, whether my own expectations for their readings were like bell hooks's notion of the jungle safari ("look students, see how noble these poor white folks are!"). But as the class unfolded, I saw how students' readings affirmed the author's desire not to romanticize, mythologize, or to "edit" the poor (Allison, 1994, p. 17) but to "make [her] world believable to people who have never experienced it" (p. 14). Allison continues:

> I was born into a world that despises the poor. . . . I know that some things must be felt to be understood, that despair, for example, can never be adequately analyzed; it must be lived. But if I can write a story that so draws the reader in that she imagines herself like my characters, feels their sense

of fear and uncertainty, their hopes and terrors, then I have come closer to knowing myself as real, important as the very people I have always watched with awe. (p. 14)

Students were, of course, stunned by the stepfather Daddy Glen's repeated molestation of Bone beginning when she was 6 years old, culminating in the heinous scene near the end of the story when he rapes her on the living room floor. But they seemed more drawn to the total fabric of the Boatwrights' lives in which these events were embedded, rather than thinking of the family as the "they" people talk about when speaking of the poor: "*They*, those people over there, those people who are not us, they die so easily, kill each other so casually. They are different" (Allison, 1994, p. 13). Similar to the public discourse demonizing unmarried teenage mothers, blaming victims of acquaintance rape, or dismissing women who "refuse" to leave their batterers, such thinking often distinguishes between the "ungrateful poor" (people like the Boatwrights), who are not worthy of attention, and their kin the "grateful poor" ("hardworking, ragged but clean, and intrinsically honorable" [Allison, 1994]), who are.

So if the Boatwrights were so unworthy—they were clearly the "ungrateful poor"—why do we as readers admire their ferocious loyalty to one another, respect their stubborn endurance of hard times, and excuse their repetitive, predictable failures? After all, Boatwright men were drunks and didn't work much; Boatwright women were always pregnant (usually before marriage) and quickly became "worn, fat, and old from working too many hours and bearing too many children"; Boatwright children eventually "quit school, stole cars, used drugs, and took dead-end jobs pumping gas or waiting tables" (Allison, 1994, p. 18).

I think the answer lies somewhere in those moments when the readers *become* the book, when we see the Boatwrights and other Others not as exotic creatures living outside our experience but as people who share our own fears and uncertainties, hopes and terrors. When we find ourselves touched at how deep a family love goes, how stubbornly families defend one another so that impulses for contempt spark what Allison calls "countersurges of pride" (1994, p. 15). When we find ourselves in awe at the wisdom of young Bone who, instead of raging at her mother's abandonment, comes to an aching understanding of the inevitable course of a Boatwright woman's life:

Who had Mama been, what had she wanted to be or do before I was born? Once I was born, her hopes had turned, and I had climbed up her life like a flower reaching for the sun. Fourteen and terrified, fifteen and a mother, just past twenty-one when she married Glen. Her life had folded into mine. What would I be like when I was fifteen, twenty, thirty? Would I be as strong as she had been, as hungry for love, as desperate, determined, and ashamed? (Allison, 1993, p. 309)

These are what I have come to believe are grace-filled pedagogic moments in the medical academy, the source of such grace being unimportant. In fact, these experiences need not even be called *grace; permeability* or *receptivity* work, too (though I like *grace* best). It has to do with all of our beliefs becoming malleable to literature—to the unfamiliar, foreign, puzzling characters and ideas found in stories—that gives me hope, a hope that such receptivity will also take place with *real* people in examining rooms, with people who are the They, the Other . . . with the Boatwrights.

The uncomfortable and cyclopean question remains: What is to be done?
—Donna Haraway, *Women Writing Culture*

Throughout this book I have attempted to theorize power and privilege on multiple levels, enacted in myriad ways, in medical education. Grounded in an academic life, I know my potential to become part of the scholarly publishing hustle involving ideology. That is, I think I know the difference between talking the talk—the uncritical appropriation of significant work on power and privilege, and walking the talk—situating our work within a dialogical relationship between ourselves and the community for whom our research, allegedly, is designed (Yeatman, 1994). I also recognize the personal and career benefits gained from writing on such charged subjects and realize, like Sleeter and McLaren (1995), that "had doors of privilege not been opened to me at points all the way through my life, I might not be in the position today to write and teach" (p. 22). Still, this writing project and others like it, woven throughout the dailiness of my teaching and other work in a medical school, are the best things I can "do," for now, with the privileged position I inhabit.

As I write these final words, I return to my original (and continued) intent for this book—to identify ways of enacting our commitment to social change that do not lead to the silence of despair or anger, or to recitations of ideology and scripted responses so easily dismissed by those who benefit from the status quo. Still, I recognize how "meticulously women take care, make nice, and rarely, in our research, express outrage at the gendered politics of [our] lives"; how we still "smuggle our knowledge of social injustice into a discourse of science that fundamentally contains, and painfully undermines, the powerful politics of activist feminism" (Fine, 1994, pp. 13–14).

"Beyond silences and scripts" does not, however, dismiss the power of silence or of ideology: There is the silence born of dissent, and the disruptive promise of theorizing women's lives. What I have tried to show here is how feminist theory and practice can be vitally grounded in the daily routines of women's work as academics; how struggles against patriarchic practices are "waged on the terrain of the classroom, the faculty and committee meeting, the office" (Luke & Gore, 1992, p. 209). I know that for every story I tell, there are countless other women telling each other stories . . . or keeping their mouths shut. Women *do* discuss these issues a lot, but they often do so in private; academic communities almost never admit complicity in oppressive practices that support and sustain the subordination of women.

In short, I have tried to add to what Michelle Fine (1994) calls the "delicious but troubling stew of theory, politics, research, and activism" (p. 31). Immersed in this simmering pot of collective struggle, women in the medical academy can both use and break silences, question what appears so natural, and forge connections between the taken-for-granted and the way things could be.

A feminist in the medical academy can work toward no less.

Notes

CHAPTER 1

1. This is odd. Medicine itself, according to Kathryn Montgomery Hunter (1991), is "fundamentally narrative" from what patients tell their doctors, to how doctors fit those details into a "narrative taxonomy of similar cases," to the written medical record, to the oral case presentation (p. 5).

CHAPTER 2

1. I am indebted here to Elizabeth Ellsworth's (1993) characterization of her various selves in "Claiming the Tenured Body."

CHAPTER 4

1. Like the royal "we," I hesitate to use the inclusive "they": Medical students, along with third-generation feminists, cannot be neatly packaged into one set of beliefs. With an apology to the diversity found in both groups, I speak of trends based on my experience in my own setting and what I have read on third-generation feminism and backlash literature.

2. I am indebted to my friend Skip Nelson, MD, who was the first person I heard use this term.

CHAPTER 5

1. My use of the term *racism* includes what van Dijk (1993) calls ethnicism, which is a system of dominance that categorizes, differentiates, and excludes persons because of "language, religion, customs, or worldviews" (p. 5).

2. Further distinctions can be made in essentialist thinking, what Locke called *real* and *nominal* essentialism. Real essence is that which is irreducible and unchanging about something; nominal essence is merely a "linguistic convenience, a classificatory fiction we need to categorize and to label. Real essences are discovered . . . nominal essences [are] assigned or produced" (Fuss, 1989, pp. 4–5). Many feminists and other groups working for social change in U.S. culture

find the concept of nominal essence useful, enabling them to hold onto group identification for political purposes without submitting to the idea that they are bound by "natural" attributes to other members of the group.

3. I'm stuck here. I could invert the hierarchy in the white/nonwhite dualism: persons with color/persons without color, trying to shift whiteness from the privileged site of normality. But, of course, white *is* a color, a sociopolitical construction. So I use "white" and "nonwhite" problematically and try to avoid "persons of color" for its implications of white-as-no-color. I'm not comfortable with any of these terms.

4. 1990 U.S. Census data indicate the following categories of licensed physicians currently practicing in the U.S.: 80.5% white, 10.8% Asian, 4.9% Hispanic, 3.6% Black, 0.1% American Indian/Eskimo, and 0.1% other race. The Census Bureau designates these categories and makes no further distinctions within them.

5. This assertion on doctor privilege I borrow from Peggy Macintosh's (1993) observation of white privilege, found in "White Privilege: Unpacking the Invisible Knapsack" (p. 210).

CHAPTER 7

1. By "province of the humanities" I do not wish to imply that everyone who lives there shares the same goals or has the same pedagogical orientation. Indeed, there are those in the medical humanities who, suffering from science- or doctor-envy, position themselves as unflinchingly hard-nosed as they can be. That is, a mean spirit can be found anywhere in the academy.

CHAPTER 8

1. The names and circumstances surrounding this situation were significantly changed to protect Rebecca as well as to take into account other issues involving confidentiality.

2. I owe this thought to the title of a book chapter by Lucy Candib, MD (1993), entitled "How Medicine Tried to Make a Man Out of Me (And Failed, Finally)."

References

Alcoff, Linda, & Potter, Elizabeth. (1993). When feminisms intersect epistemology. In Linda Alcoff & Elizabeth Potter (Eds.), *Feminist epistemologies* (pp. 1–14). New York: Routledge.

Allison, Dorothy. (1993). *Bastard out of Carolina.* New York: Plume.

Allison, Dorothy. (1994). *Skin: Talking about sex, class & literature.* Ithaca, NY: Firebrand Books.

Alvarez, Julia. (1992). *How the Garcia girls lost their accents.* New York: Plume.

American Medical Association (AMA). (1992). *Diagnostic and treatment guidelines on child sexual abuse.* Chicago: Author.

Anzaldua, Gloria. (Ed.). (1990). *Making face, making soul: Creative and critical perspectives by feminists of color.* San Francisco: Aunt Lute Books.

Apple, Michael. (1992). The text and cultural politics. *Educational Researcher, 21,* 4–11.

Baldwin, De Witt C., Daugherty, Steven R., & Eckenfels, Edward J. (1991). Student perceptions of mistreatment and harassment during medical school: A survey of ten United States schools. *Western Journal of Medicine, 155*(2), 140–145.

Banks, Joanne Trautmann. (1982). The wonders of literature in medical education. *Mobius, 2*(3), 23–31.

Bell, Derrick. (1994). *Confronting authority: Reflections of an ardent protester.* Boston: Beacon.

Beverly, Elizabeth, & Fox, Richard. (1989). Liberals must confront the conservative argument: Teaching humanities means teaching about values. *Chronicle of Higher Education, 36*(9), 52.

Bickel, Janet, Galbraith, Aarolyn, & Quinnie, Renee. (1995). *Women in academic medicine.* Washington, DC: Association of American Medical Colleges.

Bogdan, Deanne. (1994). When is a singing school (not) a chorus? The emancipatory agenda in feminist pedagogy and literature education. In Lynda Stone (Ed.), *The education feminist reader* (pp. 349–358). New York: Routledge.

Bordo, Susan. (1990). Feminism, postmodernism, and gender-scepticism. In Linda Nicholson (Ed.), *Feminism/postmodernism* (pp. 133–156). New York: Routledge.

Bordo, Susan (1994). *Unbearable weight.* Berkeley: University of California Press.

Bourdieu, Pierre. (1977). *Outline of a theory of practice* (Richard Nice, Trans.). Cambridge, UK: Cambridge University Press.

Brookner, Jackie. (1991). Feminism and students of the 80's and 90's. *Art Journal, 50*(2), 11–13.

Broyard, Anatole. (1990, April 1). Good books about being sick. *The New York Times Magazine,* pp. 1, 28–29.

Broyard, Anatole. (1992, August 26). Doctor, talk to me. *The New York Times Magazine,* pp. 33, 36.

Butler, Sandra, & Rosenblum, Barbara. (1991). *Cancer in two voices.* San Francisco: Spinsters Book Co.

Calvino, Italo. (1986). *The uses of fiction* (Patrick Creagh, Trans.). San Diego: Harcourt Brace Jovanovich.

Candib, Lucy. (1993). How medicine tried to make a man out of me (and failed, finally). In Delese Wear (Ed.), *Women in medical education: An anthology of experience* (pp. 135–144). Albany: State University of New York Press.

Carr, Rey A. (1991). Addicted to power: Sexual harassment and the unethical behaviour of university faculty. *Canadian Journal of Counselling, 25*(4), 447–461.

Cassell, Joan. (1996). The woman in the surgeon's body. *American Anthropologist, 98*(1), 41–53.

Cleage, Pearl. (1993). *Deals with the devil.* New York: Ballantine.

Code, Lorraine. (1993). Taking subjectivity into account. In Linda Alcoff & Elizabeth Potter (Eds.), *Feminist epistemologies* (pp. 15–48). New York: Routledge.

Coles, Robert. (1986). Literature and medicine. *Journal of the American Medical Association, 256,* 2125–2126.

Conley, Frances. (1993). Toward a more perfect world—Eliminating sexual discrimination in academic medicine. *New England Journal of Medicine, 328,* 351–352.

Coulehan, Jack. (1992). Teaching the patient's story. *Qualitative Health Review, 2,* 358–366.

Cowan, Gloria, Mestlin, Monja, & Masek, Julie. (1992). Predictors of feminist self-labeling. *Sex Roles, 27,* 321–330.

Craige, Betty Jean. (1992). The old order changeth . . . *Women's Review of Books, 9*(5), 14–15.

Denfeld, Rene. (1995). *The new Victorians: A young woman's challenge to the old feminist order.* New York: Warner.

Donald, James, & Rattansi, Ali. (1992). *"Race", culture and difference.* London: Sage.

Dorris, Michael. (1987). *A yellow raft in blue water.* New York: Warner.

Ehrhart, Julie, & Sandler, Bernice. (1990). *Rx for success: Improving the climate for women in medical schools and teaching hospitals.* Washington, DC: Project on the Status and Education of Women, Association of American Colleges.

Ellsworth, Elizabeth. (1989). Why doesn't this feel empowering? Working through the repressive myths of critical pedagogy. *Harvard Educational Review, 59,* 297–324.

Ellsworth, Elizabeth. (1993). Claiming the tenured body. In Delese Wear (Ed.), *The center of the web: Women and solitude* (pp. 63–74). Albany, NY: State University of New York Press.

Faludi, Susan. (1991). *Backlash: The undeclared war against American women.* New York: Crown.

Farley, Monica M., & Kozarsky, Phyllis. (1993). Sexual harassment in medical training. *New England Journal of Medicine, 329,* 661.

Feminist Majority Foundation. (1991). *Empowering women in medicine* (Empowering Women Series, No. 2). Washington, DC: Author.

Fine, Michelle. (1994). Dis-stance and other stances: Negotiations of power inside feminist research. In Andrew Gitlin (Ed.), *Power and method: Political activism and educational research* (pp. 13–35). New York: Routledge.

Fisher, Sue. (1993). Gender, power, resistance: Is care the remedy? In Sue Fisher & Kathy David (Eds.), *Negotiating at the margins: The gendered discourse of power and resistance* (pp. 87–121). New Brunswick, NJ: Rutgers University Press.

Fiske, John. (1995). Popular culture. In Frank Lentricchia & Thomas McLaughlin (Eds.), *Critical terms for literary study* (pp. 321–335). Chicago: University of Chicago Press.

Foucault, Michel. (1977). The political function of the intellectual. *Radical Philosophy, 17,* 12–14.

Freire, Paulo, & Macedo, Donald. (1995). A dialogue: Culture, language, and race. *Harvard Educational Review, 65,* 377–402.

Fuss, Diana. (1989). *Essentially speaking.* New York: Routledge.

Gallop, Jane. (1988). *Thinking through the body.* New York: Columbia University Press.

Giroux, Henry. (1992). *Border crossings: Cultural workers and the politics of education.* New York: Routledge.

Gordon, Geoffry H., Labby, Daniel, & Levinson, Wendy. (1992). Sex and the teacher–learner relationship in medicine. *Journal of General Internal Medicine, 7,* 497–505.

Gornick, Vivian. (1996). Why memoir now? *The Women's Review of Books, 13*(10–11), 5.

Gough, Noel. (1995, September). *Curriculum visions: Futures and fictions.* Paper presented at the *Journal of Curriculum Theorizing* Conference on Curriculum Theory and Classroom Practice, Monteagle, TN.

Graham, Jorie. (1980). The way things work. In Jorie Graham, *Hybrids of plants and of ghosts.* Princeton, NJ: Princeton University Press.

Grant, Linda. (1988). The gender climate of medical school: Perspectives of women and men students. *Journal of the American Medical Women's Association, 43,* 109–119.

Greene, Gayle. (1993). Looking at history. In Gayle Greene & Coppélia Kahn (Eds.), *Changing subjects: The making of feminist literary criticism* (pp. 4–27). London: Routledge.

Greene, Maxine. (1987). Sense-making through story: An autobiographical inquiry. *Teaching Education, 1*(2), 9–14.

Greene, Maxine. (1988). *The dialectic of freedom.* New York: Teachers College Press.

Greene, Maxine. (1994). Epistemology and educational research: The influence of recent approaches to knowledge. *Review of Research in Education, 20,* 423–464.

Grosz, Elizabeth. (1993). Bodies and knowledge: Feminism and the crisis of reason. In L. Alcoff & Elizabeth Potter (Eds.), *Feminist epistemologies* (pp. 187–216). New York: Routledge.

Grosz, Elizabeth. (1994). *Volatile bodies: Toward a corporeal feminism.* Bloomington: Indiana University Press.

Grumet, Madeline. (1988). *Bitter milk: Women and teaching.* Amherst: University of Massachusetts Press.

Haraway, Donna. (1995). Foreword to Gary Olson & Elizabeth Hirsh (Eds.), *Women writing culture* (pp. xi–xiii). Albany: State University of New York Press.

Harding, Sandra. (1991). *Whose knowledge? Whose science? Thinking from women's lives.* Ithaca, NY: Cornell University Press.

Hennessy, Rosemary. (1993). *Materialist feminism and the politics of discourse.* New York: Routledge.

Henry, Sherrye. (1994). *The deep divide: Why American women resist equality.* New York: Macmillan.

Heshusius, Lous. (1994). Freeing ourselves from objectivity: Managing subjectivity or turning toward a participatory mode of consciousness? *Educational Researcher, 23*(3), 15–22.

Hilfiker, David. (1989). Facing brokenness. *Second Opinion, 11,* 92–107.

Hite, Molly. (1993). "Except thou ravish mee": Penetrations into the life of the (feminine) mind. In Gayle Greene & Coppélia Kahn (Eds.), *Changing subjects: The making of feminist literary criticism* (pp. 121–128). London: Routledge.

Holmes, Helen B. (1992). A call to heal medicine. In Helen B. Holmes & Aura Purdy (Eds.), *Feminist perspectives in medical ethics* (pp. 1–8). Bloomington: Indiana University Press.

hooks, bell. (1990). *Yearning: Race, gender, and cultural politics.* Boston: South End Press.

hooks, bell. (1992). Out of the academy and into the streets. *Ms., 3*(1), 80–82.

hooks, bell. (1994a). *Teaching to transgress: Education as the practice of freedom.* New York: Routledge.

hooks, bell. (1994b). *Outlaw culture: Resisting representations.* New York: Routledge.

hooks, bell, & West, Cornel. (1991). *Breaking bread: Insurgent black intellectual life.* Boston: South End Press.

Hostler, Sharon L., & Gressard, Risa P. (1993). Perceptions of the gender fairness of the medical education environment. *Journal of the American Medical Women's Association, 48,* 51–54.

Hunter, Kathryn Montgomery. (1991). *Doctor stories: The narrative structure of medical knowledge.* Princeton, NJ: Princeton University Press.

Jaggar, Alison. (1992). Love and knowledge: Emotion in feminist epistemology. In Elizabeth Harvey & Kathleen Okruhlik (Eds.), *Women and reason* (pp. 115–142). Ann Arbor: University of Michigan Press.

Johnson, F. L. (1993). Women's leadership in higher education: Is the agenda feminist? *College and University Personnel Association Journal, 44,* 12.

Kaminer, Wendy. (1990). *A fearful freedom: Women's flight from equality.* Reading, MA: Addison-Wesley.

Kaminer, Wendy. (1995, June 4). Feminism's third wave: What do young women want? *The New York Times Book Review,* pp. 3, 22–23.

Komaromy, Miriam, Bindman, Andrew, Haber, Richard, & Sande, Merle. (1993). Sexual harassment in medical training. *New England Journal of Medicine, 328,* 322–326.

Lather, Patti. (1986). Issues of validity in openly ideological research: Between a rock and a soft place. *Interchange, 17*(4), 63–84.

Lather, Patti. (1991). *Getting smart: Feminist research and pedagogy within the postmodern.* New York: Routledge.

Lather, Patti. (1994). Dada practice: A feminist reading. *Curriculum Inquiry, 24*(2), 181–187.

Lenhart, Sharon, Klein, Freada, Falcao, Patricia, Phelan, Elizabeth, & Smith, Kevin. (1991). Gender bias against and sexual harassment of AMWA members in Massachusetts. *Journal of the American Medical Women's Association, 46,* 121–125.

Lewis, Magda. (1990). Interrupting patriarchy: Politics, resistance, and transformation in the feminist classroom. *Harvard Educational Review, 60*(4), 467–488.

Lewis, Magda. (1993). *Without a word: Reaching beyond women's silence.* New York: Routledge.

Lewis, Magda, & Simon, Roger. (1986). A discourse not intended for her: Learning and teaching within patriarchy. *Harvard Educational Review, 56*(4), 457–472.

Long, Priscilla. (1992). Writing for our lives. *The Women's Review of Books, 9*(5), 1, 3–4.

Luke, Carmen, & Gore, Jennifer. (1992). Women in the academy: Strategy, struggle, survival. In Carmen Luke & Jennifer Gore (Eds.), *Feminisms and critical pedagogy* (pp. 192–210). New York: Routledge.

Macintosh, Peggy. (1993). White privilege: Unpacking the invisible knapsack. In Virginia Cyrus (Ed.), *Experiencing race, class, and gender in the United States* (pp. 209–212). Mountain View, CA: Mayfield Publications.

Mairs, Nancy. (1994). *Voice lessons.* Boston: Beacon.

Marshall, Brenda. (1992). *Teaching the postmodern: Fiction and theory.* New York: Routledge.

McCarthy, Cameron. (1993). After the canon: Knowledge and ideological representation in the multicultural discourse on curriculum reform. In Cameron McCarthy & Warren Crichlow (Eds.), *Race, identity, and representation in education* (pp. 289–305). New York: Routledge.

Messer-Davidow, Ellen. (1989). The philosophical bases of feminist literary criticisms. In Linda Kauffman (Ed.), *Gender and theory: Dialogues on feminist criticism* (pp. 63–106). Oxford: Blackwell.

Miller, Nancy K. (1991). *Getting personal: Feminist occasions and other autobiographical acts.* New York: Routledge.

Minh-ha, Trinh T. (1989). *Women native other.* Bloomington: Indiana University Press.

Mishler, Elliot. (1984). *The discourse of medicine: Dialectics of medical interviews.* Norwood, NJ: Ablex.

Morrison, Toni. (1970). *The bluest eye.* New York: Simon & Schuster.

Mueller, Lisel. (1986). Why we tell stories. In Lisel Mueller, *The need to hold still* (pp. 62–63). Baton Rouge: Louisiana State University Press.

Mukherjee, Bharati. (1991). A four-hundred-year-old woman. In Philomena Mariani (Ed.), *Critical fictions: The politics of imaginative writing* (pp. 24–28). Seattle: Bay Press.

Naylor, Gloria. (1982). *The women of Brewster Place.* New York: Viking.

Nora, Lois. (1996). Sexual harassment in medical education: A review of the literature with comments from the law. *Academic Medicine, 71*(1), 113–118.

Olds, Sharon. (1984). Miscarriage. In Sharon Olds, *The dead and the living*. New York: Knopf.

Pagano, Jo Anne. (1990). *Exiles and communities: Teaching in the patriarchal wilderness*. Albany: State University of New York Press.

Paglia, Camille. (1992). *Sex, art, and American culture: Essays*. New York: Vintage.

Paglia, Camille. (1994). *Vamps & tramps: New essays*. New York: Vintage.

Pastan, Linda. (1982). Notes from the delivery room. In Linda Pastan, *PM/AM: New and selected poems*. New York: Norton.

Pellegrino, Edward. (1980). To look feelingly—The affinities of medicine in literature. In E. Peschel (Ed.), *Medicine in literature* (pp. xv–xix). New York: Watson.

Percy, Walker. (1971). *Love in the ruins*. New York: Farrar, Straus, & Giroux.

Pinar, William, Reynolds, William, Slattery, Patrick, & Taubman, Peter. (Eds.). (1995). *Understanding curriculum*. New York: Peter Lang.

Poirier, Suzanne, & Brauner, Daniel. (1988). Ethics and the daily language of medical discourse. *Hastings Center Report, 18*(4), 5–9.

Pomorska, Krystyna. (1984). Forward. In Mikhail Bakhtin, *Rabelais and his world* (Hélène Iswolsky, Trans.). Bloomington: Indiana University Press.

Pressman, Sarah. (1991). The numbers do not add up to equality. *Journal of the American Medical Women's Association, 46*, 44.

Rich, Adrienne. (1978). *On lies, secrets, and silence*. New York: Norton.

Rich, Adrienne. (1979). Disloyal to civilization. In Adrienne Rich, *On lies, secrets, and silence* (pp. 275–310). New York: Norton.

Rich, Adrienne. (1984). The burning of paper instead of children. In Adrienne Rich, *The fact of a doorframe* (pp. 116–119). New York: Norton.

Rich, Adrienne. (1985). Taking women students seriously. In Margo Culley & Catherine Portuges (Eds.), *Gendered subjects: The dynamics of feminist teaching* (pp. 21–28). Boston: Routledge & Kegan Paul.

Riger, Stephanie. (1991). Gender dilemmas in sexual harassment policies and procedures. *American Psychologist, 46*, 497–505.

Ritchie, Mary. (1995). Whose voice is it anyway?: Vocalizing multicultural analysis. In Christine Sleeter & Peter McClaren (Eds.), *Multicultural education, critical pedagogy, and the politics of difference* (pp. 309–316). Albany: State University of New York Press.

Robinson, Lillian. (1978). *Sex, class, and culture*. Bloomington: Indiana University Press.

Roiphe, Katie. (1993). *The morning after: Sex, fear, and feminism on campus*. Boston: Little, Brown.

Roman, Leslie. (1993). White is a color! White defensiveness, postmodernism, and anti-racist pedagogy. In Cameron McCarthy & Warren Crichlow (Eds.), *Race, identity, and representation in education* (pp. 71–88). New York: Routledge.

Rushdie, Salman. (1990). *Is nothing sacred?* (The Herbert Read Memorial Lecture). London: Granta.

Russo, Mary. (1986). Female grotesques: Carnival and theory. In Teresa de Lauretis (Ed.), *Feminist studies/critical studies* (pp. 213–229). Bloomington: Indiana University Press.

Said, Edward. (1989). Representing the colonized: Anthropology's interlocutors. *Critical Inquiry, 15,* 195–226.

Said, Edward. (1993). *Culture and imperialism.* New York: Knopf.

Sarup, Madan. (1993). *An introductory guide to post-structuralism and postmodernism.* (2nd ed.). Athens: University of Georgia Press.

Schwartz, Lynne Sharon. (1987). So you're going to have a new body! In *The melting pot (and other subversive stories)* (pp. 42–58). New York: Harper & Row.

Schweickart, Patrocinio. (1986). Reading ourselves: Toward a feminist theory of reading. In Elizabeth Flynn & Patrocinio Schweickart (Eds.), *Gender and reading: Essays on readers, texts, and contexts* (pp. 31–62). Baltimore: Johns Hopkins University Press.

Sherwin, Susan. (1992a). *No longer patient: Feminist ethics and health care.* Philadelphia: Temple University Press.

Sherwin, Susan. (1992b). Feminist and medical ethics: Two different approaches to contextual ethics. In Helen Holmes & Laura Purdy (Eds.), *Feminist perspectives in medical ethics* (pp. 17–31). Bloomington: Indiana University Press.

Sleeter, Christine, & McLaren, Peter (Eds.). (1995). *Multicultural education, critical pedagogy, and the politics of difference.* Albany: State University of New York Press.

Smiley, Jane. (1991). *A thousand acres.* New York: Knopf.

Snow, C. P. (1959). *The two cultures.* Cambridge: Cambridge University Press.

Sternhell, Carol. (1994). The proper study of womankind. *Women's Review of Books, 12*(3), 1–3.

Tanenbaum, Leora. (1995). Divide and conquer? *Women's Review of Books, 12* (3), 5–6.

Tillman, Lynne. (1991). Critical fiction/critical self. In Philomena Mariani (Ed.), *Critical fiction: The politics of imaginative writing* (pp. 97–103). Seattle: Bay Press.

Tompkins, Jane. (1989). Me and my shadow. In Linda Kaufmann (Ed.), *Gender and theory: Dialogues in feminist criticism* (pp. 121–139). Oxford: Blackwell.

van Dijk, Teun A. (1993). *Elite discourse and racism.* Newbury Park, CA: Sage.

Verghese, Abraham. (1994). *My own country: A doctor's story of a town and its people in the age of* AIDS. New York: Simon & Schuster.

Waitzkin, Howard. (1991). *The politics of medical encounters: How patients and doctors deal with social problems.* New Haven, CT: Yale University Press.

Walker, Alice. (1973). In these dissenting times. In Alice Walker, *Revolutionary petunias & other poems.* New York: Harcourt Brace.

Walker, Alice. (1979). At first. In Alice Walker, *Good night, Willie Lee.* New York: Doubleday.

Walker, Alice. (1982). *The color purple.* New York: Simon & Schuster.

Walker, R. B. J. (1988). *One world, many worlds: Struggles for a just world peace.* Boulder, CO: Lynne Rienner Publishers.

Wallace, Michele. (1993). Multiculturalism and oppositionality. In Cameron McCarthy & Warren Crichlow (Eds.), *Race, identity, and representation in education* (pp. 251–261). New York: Routledge.

Walsh, Mary Roth. (1990). Women in medicine since Flexner. *New York State Journal of Medicine, 90,* 302–308.

Warren, Virginia. (1992). Feminist directions in medical ethics. In Helen Holmes & Laura Purdy (Eds.), *Feminist perspectives in medical ethics* (pp. 32–45). Bloomington: Indiana University Press.

Welch, Sharon. (1990). *A feminist ethic of risk.* Minneapolis: Fortress.

Wicomb, Zoe. (1991). An author's agenda. In Philomena Mariani (Ed.), *Critical fictions: The politics of imaginative writing* (pp. 13–16). Seattle: Bay Press.

Williams, A. Paul, Pierre, Karin D., & Vayda, Eugene. (1993). Women in medicine: Toward a conceptual understanding of the potential for change. *Journal of the American Medical Women's Association, 48,* 115–121.

Williams, Patricia J. (1991). *The alchemy of race and rights: Diary of a law school professor.* Cambridge, MA: Harvard University Press.

Wolf, Naomi. (1993). *Fire with fire.* Toronto: Random House.

Yalom, Irvin. (1989). Fat lady. In Irvin Yalom, *Love's executioner and other tales of psychotherapy* (pp. 87–117). New York: Basic Books.

Yamato, Gloria. (1990). Something about the subject makes it hard to name. In Gloria Anzaldu (Ed.), *Making face, making soul: Creative and critical perspectives by feminists of color* (pp. 20–24). San Francisco: Aunt Lute Books.

Yeatman, Anna. (1994). Postmodern epistemological politics and social science. In Kathleen Lennon & Margaret Whitford (Eds.), *Knowing the difference: Feminist perspectives in epistemology* (pp. 187–202). London: Routledge.

Index

About the Author

DELESE WEAR is an associate professor in the Behavioral Sciences Department at the Northeastern Ohio Universities College of Medicine. She coordinates the Human Values in Medicine Program, which seeks to integrate humanities inquiry in medical education, and teaches courses on literature and medicine to medical students. She is also the Associate Director of the Women and Medicine Program. She edited *The Center of the Web: Women and Solitude* and *Women in Medical Education: An Anthology of Experience* and co-authored (with Lois LaCivita Nixon) *Literary Anatomies: Women's Bodies and Health in Literature.*